LENNOX LEWIS

LENNOX LEWIS

*The Autobiography
of the WBC Heavyweight Champion
of the World*

with
JOE STEEPLES

faber and faber
LONDON · BOSTON

First published in 1993
by Faber and Faber Limited
3 Queen Square London WC1N 3AU

Photoset in Sabon by Parker Typesetting Service, Leicester
Printed in England by Clays Ltd, St Ives plc

A CIP record for this book is available
from the British Library

ISBN 0–571–17191–5

2 4 6 8 10 9 7 5 3 1

For Violet

Contents

Illustrations

Preliminaries

Lennox Lewis is a sporting hero: the first British-born fighter to win a world heavyweight championship this century.

Britain's relationship with the world heavyweight title is a curious one, providing an insight into our national character. We've smiled through so many defeats that failure became accepted as our lot. Defeat is something we accept gracefully, good-loser smiles sutured over painful disappointment.

Since William Hazlitt wrote in 'Merrie England', about our bare-knuckle men, 'The noble science of boxing is all our own', the heavyweight division has been dominated almost exclusively by Americans.

In 1901, two years after James J. Jeffries knocked out Cornish-born Bob Fitzsimmons – the last Englishman to hold the title – A. F. Bettinson gave a talk to the National Sporting Club on 'The Decline of English Champions'. Recent defeats, he said, had been 'disconcerting to anyone not possessed of the stoicism of a Roman Senator'. But he had touching faith that the heavyweight title soon would be back where it belonged. 'Signs, indeed, point out to an eye not altogether unpractised in noting such symptoms, that as far as English boxing is concerned the moment of revival is upon us,' declared Bettinson (who, from his photograph, was a dead ringer for Buffalo Bill). 'To begin with the foundations of things and men, the form shown this year by Public Schools has been characterized by very marked improvement. At the Army Boxing Competitions the same welcome advance in the right direction has manifested itself.'

Sadly, the combined might of the British army and our public schoolboys let us down badly. The twentieth century has been marked by a cavalcade of doomed contenders. Since Fitzsimmons was beaten at Coney Island on 9 June 1899, eleven Britons have had a dozen cracks at wresting back the heavyweight title. All failed, and only two survived to the final bell. Joe Bugner back-pedalled for fifteen cautious rounds with Muhammed Ali in Kuala Lumpur in 1975. Tommy Farr put up a game, tough fight in Joe Louis' first defence of his title at Madison Square Garden on 30 August 1937. Some people at the ringside, and millions in Britain who later watched the cinema newsreels, thought Farr had done enough to win, but the verdict went to the home boy, Louis.

As for our other hopefuls, their shortcomings as they tried to fend off annihilation were sometimes laughable. A few seemed to go into the ring for their big pay-day with the strategy that the quickest way to get things over with was to lose. Roughly exposed to the Americans, our golden boys proved they weren't even gold-plated. A. J. Liebling, author of the boxing classic *The Sweet Science*, wrote in 1957, 'No great heavyweight has learned his trade in Britain within the memory of any living man under a hundred.'

The dismal record of our big men has been compensated for by a tradition of heroic failure. We nurture our also-rans, elevating them to the status of mythological lionhearts. This condition frequently leads on to a theatrical career. After Gunner Moir was knocked out by Tommy Burns in 1907, he lost eight of his next nine fights, then switched to acting, where he had great success appearing in British films in small parts such as an executioner.

Frank Bruno's bludgeonings by Tim Witherspoon and Mike Tyson led to lucrative roles in pantomime, where he played a genie and Robin Hood. Frank enjoyed himself in panto, but proved conclusively that he is better as a boxer than as a thespian – in his key scene as the genie, he was out-acted by Aladdin's lamp.

So perhaps it was only to be expected that when, at last, we laid claim to a genuine share in the title, it happened against a background of high farce.

Lennox Lewis became heavyweight champion of the world while on holiday in Jamaica. Since many people believe that boxing should carry a government health warning, winning the supreme prize in sport's rawest competition while caressed by the soothing zephyrs of a Caribbean winter seems like nice work if you can get it.

But Lennox, clearly the most potent heavyweight Britain has had this century, was begrudged his cushy triumph. There were snide comments, particularly from across the Atlantic, about the way in which our first heavyweight champion for ninety-four years came by his World Boxing Council title.

Comparisons were made with the German Max Schmeling, who in 1930 became champion while lying groaning on the ring floor of the Yankee Stadium. Schmeling won the title after a low blow from Jack Sharkey left him writhing on the canvas. *Unser* Max became the first challenger to win the title dumped on his rump. (In 1936 he also became the only mortal ever to knock out Joe Louis, earning himself a telegram from the Führer: 'Your victory is a German victory. We are proud of you. Heil Hitler and hearty greetings.')

Jim Murray of the *Los Angeles Times* scoffed, 'Schmeling became champion by default. Lewis became the champion by phone.' At least Max had won the title in the ring, or as he was being carried out of it. But Lennox hadn't even worn gloves and gum-shield when his WBC belt was conferred: he heard he was world champion in December 1992 while relaxing on Trial Bay Golf Course, just down the road from Montego.

The news made Mr Murray apoplectic. 'Nothing, it seems, can prevent the spread of the title by registered letter, voice mail or cablegram,' he grumbled.

(The only other heavyweight to win a world title outside the ring was Ken Norton. He was proclaimed champion by the WBC in 1978 after it disapproved of Muhammed Ali defending his title against Leon Spinks on 15 February 1978.)

But the absurdity of being given a title without breaking sweat has more to do with the peculiar circumstances of world boxing than with Lewis's championship credentials.

When Lennox demolished Donovan 'Razor' Ruddock in 226 seconds of raw action on Halloween 1992, he expected to get first shot at the winner of the 13 November Evander Holyfield–Riddick Bowe title bout. It was an agreement both Holyfield and Bowe had signed their names to.

But when Bowe outpointed Holyfield over twelve blisteringly ferocious rounds, it soon became clear that Rock Newman, Bowe's manager, had no immediate plans for his man to get into the ring with Lewis. Lennox had shown how dangerous he was when he clobbered Bowe to defeat in the second round of the super-heavyweight final at the Seoul Olympics in 1988. After the medal ceremony in Korea, Bowe, still smarting at losing the gold medal, told Lewis, 'See you in the pros.'

But once he became undisputed heavyweight champion, the last person he wanted to see in the pros at that precise moment was Lewis. There were millions of easier dollars to be made first, by fighting lesser men.

Newman appeared to have about as much intention of allowing Bowe to face Lennox right away as he had of playing baseball with a hand-grenade. Why risk messing with live ammunition when he could offer his fighter spent bullets? Michael Dokes, whose biggest fight in the 1980s was against cocaine addiction, lasted 2 minutes 19 seconds in Bowe's first defence of the title in February 1993. According to the *Washington Post*, he was 'So far past his prime, he had to take a cab back'. Jesse Ferguson, Bowe's opponent in May, ring-frayed and long past his sell-by date, did what could be expected of a 40–1 underdog. He was knocked out in the seventeenth second of round two.

It was knock-about stuff of a different calibre the previous December. The circus of the Bowe entourage had rolled into London for the BBC's *Sports Personality of the Year* programme, and very soon the clowns were loosed into the arena.

While he was here Bowe called a press conference at which he renounced his WBC title. Wearing an off-white suit sawn off at the knees that made him look like a cross between Colonel Sanders and Orson Welles, Rock Newman stage-managed the dumping of the WBC belt into a rubbish bin.

The stunt was pulled in a wood-panelled room in London's St James Court Hotel. Bowe and Newman must have known they were going to be stripped of the WBC crown because of their reluctance to meet Lewis, so they prepared their flamboyant little tableau. As far as they were concerned, it was a case of trash the WBC belt before the WBC trashed them. Beating the WBC to the punch, Bowe declared, 'As long as I remain champion I will not be involved with any part of the WBC, and today I am withdrawing my recognition of them.'

(It wasn't even the real WBC belt, but a replica they had recently purchased from Evander Holyfield. Even so, they made sure they retrieved the fake from the bin after their photo-call.)

Meanwhile a van-load of men dressed as chickens paraded on the pavement outside the hotel. They had been hired by Lewis's manager, Frank Maloney – or 'Frankly Baloney' as he was referred to by Bowe – to cast aspersions on the courage of the American heavyweight.

It was all very silly – typical of the showmen and hucksters who fulminate around the flashy world of boxing. Soon it degenerated into mere name-calling. 'Lennox Lewis is a legend in his own mind,' said Newman. 'He is a household name only in his own household.'

Bowe pointed his chipolata fingers at the belt languishing in the folds of a green bin-liner and sneered, 'If Lennox wants that, we can call Lennox the garbage-picker.' (Some garbage-picker. His first defence of the WBC title earned Lewis $9 million.)

The same day the WBC reacted swiftly and angrily from its headquarters in Mexico City. 'The belt thrown into the trash bin has been worn with dignity and pride by Muhammed Ali, Larry Holmes and Mike Tyson,' huffed the Council's planet-shaped president Jose Sulaiman. 'We expected that Bowe would try to duck the winner of

Lewis and Ruddock. Bowe has reneged on his agreement to fight Lewis. He is running scared.'

While Bowe's chickens flew home to roost, Lennox was left to reflect that all the byzantine intrigue had gifted him the key to a fortune. His arrival at a pinnacle of his sport may have been a bloodless anticlimax. But with a world title – even only one of the four sets of initials on offer – he is a precious commodity. Lennox now has access to the most extraordinary earning-machine in sport. His contract with Home Box Office, the American cable television company, promises to launch him into the richest career ever essayed by a sportsman from this country.

Like an amoeba, the heavyweight title has come apart. There are now three men sharing portions of the world heavyweight crown. Bowe retains the World Boxing Association and International Boxing Federation titles, Lennox is the World Boxing Council's champion, and Tommy Morrison, the white hope from Kansas, is the World Boxing Organization's claimant. Sorting out the first among these alleged equals will make them all very rich.

The difficulty is that, while soccer has FIFA (the Fédération Inter-nationale de Football Association), there is no one governing body for boxing that alone has the right to organize world championships. There are so many initials involved in boxing titles that the various directorates have been described as alphabet soup. When no title is vacant or shared, sixty-eight boxers have a world-title belt in their care. This is because four world boxing associations sanction cham-pionship fights in seventeen weight divisions (see Appendix 1). When Jack Dempsey bossed the heavyweights in the 1920s there were only eight classical fighting weights and eight undisputed champions of the world. Now there are almost as many boxing champions as there are extras in a Cecil B. De Mille biblical epic.

The biggest issue in boxing right now is, Will Bowe and Lewis ever meet in the professional ring? A return fight between them promises to be an epic feat of arms, and is the one every fan most wants to see.

HBO has signed the two rivals – Bowe to a six-fight deal, Lewis to four. If they both keep winning they could meet eventually for a $100 million showdown. As Seth Abraham, the president of Time–Warner Sports, which owns HBO, says, 'I think there should be one champion. That's what the public wants. They are the jury, they pay the freight. The sooner it happens the better.

'HBO spent $25 million to unify the heavyweight championship from 1986 to 1989. It's in our best business interests to have one world champion, and the fastest way to reunify the title is to have Bowe and Lewis under contract.'

Lennox is hungry more for the undisputed title than for the huge cash jackpot. 'I don't look at the money aspect. I just look at the aspect of achieving a goal I have always worked for. I've always felt like a champion – now I just want to prove to the world that I'm a worthy champion.

'I hope Riddick doesn't get beaten before I get to him. I want him. I want to be the undisputed champion. I'm counting the days until I get to him. The count has started in my head, and I hope I get to him sooner rather than later. I'm the better man. I've known that since Seoul. I just need the opportunity to prove it one more time.'

The countdown has begun.

1

A Real Lennox

Port Antonio is the sort of place the camera loves to drool over in holiday programmes. Blue breakers pound in over great sweeps of white sand on unforgettable beaches. A swift, green river – the Rio Grande – tumbles through gorges and great tunnels of bamboo.

The town on Jamaica's north-east tip was once the major banana port, where many of the island's first tourists arrived on banana boats.

The original posters of the old shipping lines make the place appear as distant as the moon, and in the 1920s and 1930s its shabby tropical charms and faded Georgian architecture attracted visitors like Rudyard Kipling, Bette Davis, J. P. Morgan and William Randolph Hearst.

Its most passionate *habitué* was the actor Errol Flynn, lured by its vague notions of time and its exotic wickedness. He owned the 68-acre Mary Island in the harbour, tied up his yacht *Zaca* on the quay, and was a regular tourist feature on the docks, eating raw dolphin and swigging neat gin at 10.00 a.m. He even sponsored his own calypso band, Errol Flynn's Swamp Boys, who played all over the North of Jamaica.

He was captivated by the place. In his autobiography, *My Wicked Wicked Ways*, he wrote, 'Never had I seen a land so beautiful. Now I know where the writers of the Bible had got their description of paradise. They had come here to Jamaica and then their words had been set down and they have been read ever since.'

Only the visiting rich and famous enjoyed the same hedonistic lifestyle as Errol Flynn. Huddled below the grand villas and hotels were the humbler homes where most of the 11,000 population of Port Antonio lived. In one of them, with planks for walls and a zinc roof, Violet Lewis was raised by her Aunt Gee. The three-roomed house, just across the road from the dock, was called Harbour View.

Violet was born on 10 May 1938, nine miles along the coast in Boston Bay, in a house to match her father's income – very small. Her father, Cedric, was an odd-jobbing labourer whose main income came from hawking Snowballs, primitive home-made versions of what are now called Slush Puppies – drinks made by pouring fruit syrup over crushed ice – to neighbourhood children. Her mother, Margaret, was a tall, powerfully built woman – the image of her future grandson, Lennox. She added to the family's meagre income by taking in washing and ironing.

There were twelve Lewis children – seven boys and five girls – who soon outgrew the house. The family was not so poor as to be wretched, but, to help ease the overcrowding, Violet was farmed out at an early age to live with her Aunt Gee, who ran a fruit and vegetable stall in Port Antonio market. When Gee married Mr Son Baker, Vi moved on to live with another relative, Aunt Lou.

'Life was very hard for us,' Violet recalls. 'With so many children, there wasn't much money to go round, and I can't recall ever living at home with my brothers and sisters. I really hardly knew my mum and dad.

'My most vivid memories are going down to the harbour to watch all the tourists' boats. Errol Flynn had a boat there and I remember meeting him when I was a little girl. You couldn't really miss him because he was so loud.'

By the time Violet left Port Antonio High School at seventeen, Aunt Gee had already left Jamaica to set up home in the East End of

London with her husband. It was 1956, and Britain was enjoying the postwar economic boom. Viewed from the poverty of Port Antonio, England seemed like the promised land. Aunt Gee sent back a one-way air ticket, and Violet flew to Heathrow with her best friend, Hazel Harris.

'We were both young and innocent. We hadn't even seen our capital, Kingston, let alone fly on an aeroplane. Of course we were very excited and had our best clothes on to make a good impression for the big occasion. I wore a nice two-piece suit with stockings that rolled just above the knee. Very smart.'

In June 1948 when the first Jamaican immigrants arrived on the SS *Empire Windrush* they were invited to a civic tea with the mayor of Brixton. An account of their arrival in London was headlined in the *Evening Standard* 'Welcome Home.' That's just how Violet felt when she arrived – at home.

'I'd heard so much about England. We'd been brought up to regard it as the mother country. So we were all happy just to be here – never mind about the fog and the queues. That's one thing I really didn't like about this place – the queues. In Jamaica nobody ever queues.

'The impression I got when I was a youngster was that money grew on trees in England. The first pay-packet I got [she worked in an electrical-goods factory at Plaistow] was £4 12s. od. I felt I was the richest person in the world. Since it was my first wages, I had a spree and spent it all on myself. It seemed a huge amount of money to someone just over from Jamaica.

'I used to write home to my friend and tell her things were so lovely over here you could pick the money from the trees. So silly. A silly girl enjoying every minute of her new life.'

But it wasn't long before things turned sour at home. Aunt Gee began to treat her like a skivvy. Violet moved out. Over the next few years she rented rooms in a number of Victorian tenement houses converted into flats in what is now called Newham. In turn she lived in St Anthony's Road, Victoria Road, and Green Street – all close to

West Ham United Football Club, which her two sons would grow up to support.

With the move came a change of job. She became a nursing auxiliary, working at several hospitals in the East End before settling at East Ham General. Then on 27 April 1962, her elder boy, 7 lb. 7 oz. Dennis Stephen was born at Queen Mary's Hospital, Stratford. He is the son of Rupert Daries, a Jamaican swimming instructor, who now works as a masseur. (Coincidentally, one of his clients is Frank Bruno.)

Dennis was named after a television programme Violet happened to be watching while nursing him in her arms — ' "Dennis the Menace",' she says, with an engulfing laugh — 'but he hates to be reminded of it.'

She went back to her job at the hospital as soon as possible, using babyminders and Aunt Gee to look after her son when she was on night shift. 'Dennis was the best baby out. He was never a problem. He'd sleep all day, and you'd have to wake him to feed him. His dad was always very good to us. Dennis was never the problem with him — I was the problem.

'We were two very different people. I didn't like his jealousy. He was so jealous. If I went to the store he'd watch, and if I was late coming back he'd want to know where I was — he didn't like it.

'I never wanted to get married because of his jealousy. I really liked him as a brother. I had Dennis with him, but I really didn't love him. After a while I thought I might fall in love with him. You think, Well if you don't love him at first, if you live together you may grow to love him. But it never happened like that.'

Eventually he married someone else. Later, when Violet emigrated, Dennis moved in with his father and was brought up with the Daries family. 'He took very good care of Dennis. He is a very good person,' says Violet, 'I still talk to him. Once in a while he'll phone and he'll say to Dennis, "How's your mum?" You know, I think he's still carrying a torch for me.' And she laughs again, like warm molasses.

But soon Violet did find the love of her life. At a party she met another Jamaican, who worked at Fords in Dagenham. His name was Carlton Brooks.

'It turned out that he was married, but I didn't know. In those days they'd leave their wives in Jamaica while they came over here to make a better life for themselves. He never told me he was married – he strung me along. Then, when I told him I was pregnant with Lennox, he said, "I'm sorry, Vi – I'm married and I can't marry you."

'I had no idea he was married. It was a great shock for me to hear he had a family. I think he was the only man I really, really cared for. I would have married him. It made me very sad.

'We met at a party. I was madly in love with him, though we never lived together. I had my place and he had his. We didn't have a big row when he told me about his family, but I was very disappointed in him.

'The sadness is still there. That's why I don't like to talk about it. I've never told the papers all the details. It hurts so much to go over it again, as I did care for him a lot.'

To make enough to pay her bills, Violet would have to do extra shifts and work all through her pregnancy. Life was hard enough for a single mother with one toddler to care for: a second baby threatened to be a hopeless burden, especially as she had planned to study to become a state registered nurse. Violet's friends at the hospital advised her to have an abortion.

'I was thinking about it all the time. Should I abort the baby? The sister at the hospital booked an appointment for me, but I couldn't do it. I wouldn't do it. The sister knew I had a son already, and she said, "It's going to be even more difficult for you, Vi. It's going to be very hard. Think about it." But I said no.

'Then as soon as I had Lennox in my arms I knew I had made the right decision. As I cuddled him to me I knew I would never regret it, because he was so precious. And he is still precious to me twenty-eight years later.

'I suppose that is why Lennox and I are so close, because he is all I had to cling to. I did care for Carlton – that's why I poured all my love on Lennox. I don't know if it was wrong of me to do that, to show him so much love.

'In spite of all the heartache and hardships he put me through, I'm grateful to Carlton because he gave me a lovely son who is my pride and joy. He is the loser because he has missed out on the love of a marvellous boy, and I am the winner because I've got my Lennox.'

Lennox Claudius Lewis weighed in at 10 lb. 10 oz. when he arrived in the world by Caesarean section at the same hospital where Dennis was born, Queen Mary's, Stratford, on 2 September 1965.

His first name was given him by the doctor who delivered him. Violet chose the second because it had an imperious Roman ring about it. He took Violet's surname because the fourth space on his birth certificate, where the name of the father usually goes, remained a blank.

Purely by chance, between them they chose perfectly for a child destined to earn his living with his fists. 'Lennox', from the Gaelic, means 'chieftain'. Claudius was the Roman emperor who in AD 43 conquered Britain,. And the surname 'Lewis' is an Anglo-French form of the old Frankish 'Hludwig', meaning 'loud battle'.

Lennox lived up to all his names, boisterously waving his fists and making lusty noises as the doctor wrapped him in a blanket and put him to his mother's breast.

'I didn't know why the doctor chose Lennox, or what it meant. He just came up to my bed and said, "You've got a Lennox there. He's a real Lennox." He didn't explain why, and I didn't think of asking him why, but it sounded right so that's what I called him,' says Violet.

From day one Lennox was a strong, vigorous child. 'If you went into the hospital nursery all the other babies would be lying still and quiet, wrapped up in their shawls. But Lennox, I swear it, would be lifting up his head to look at you. He's always been very big and full of energy.'

When Violet brought her new son home to Victoria Road, the forebodings of her colleagues at work were proved correct. It was back-breaking work bringing up two young boys and coping with night shifts. But she managed, with the help of Aunt Gee, numerous childminders, and the fathers of her sons. 'They always did everything possible to help,' she says. 'To tell you the truth, they both looked out for the boys as much as they could.'

No one should misread Violet as lax or feckless – she simply fell in love and it didn't go all according to script. Now she is comfortably mellowing into middle age, a pillar of her local Pentecostal church, and hankers for her sons to give her grandchildren. (She has already chosen a list of suitable names.) But it is easy to look beyond today's warm-hearted maternal figure and to imagine her as she was in her twenties – exuberant, true to herself, full of fun and spirit, an independent and determined young woman.

She has nothing to hang her head about. 'I suppose some people might condemn me. But my friends at work were always a great help and comfort. Looking back, I wouldn't change anything. All the hardships, all the suffering, it's been worth it in the end. I wouldn't change a moment of it. Looking back, even those hard times don't seem so hard now.

'If I could live my life again I'd make the same mistakes, because I don't look at them as mistakes. All my prayers are all answered. I have a lot to thank God for. I can see the results of all that he's done in my life, and I'm grateful.'

Still a little misty about her doomed love-affair, Violet found herself trapped in a daily routine of work, kids, work. At home she was faced with hours of slablike solitude with only babytalk to break it up. She says, 'I didn't have a life of my own. It was just work and the boys, work and the boys.' Dennis remembers the effect on the family. 'My mum seemed to be working all hours – night shifts, late work, lots of shifts at the hospital. She's always done a lot of work, and we went to different childminders so I didn't see much of Lennox. I didn't know him as a baby.'

Meanwhile Lennox's first conscious memory is of a rocking-horse. It would have echoes of Citizen Kane's Rosebud, if only he could remember what it was called. 'I used to sit on it for hours, rocking away,' he says, 'That's the first image of myself that I carry in my head.

'I remember Dennis seemed very quiet compared to me. I bugged him, because I was noisy and active. I suppose I was just like everyone's younger brother – I always wanted to play with his toys and join in his games.'

When Lennox was four and Dennis seven, Violet made a decision that was to change all their lives. The daily grind was getting her down, her existence was strenuous and unhappy, and her nerves were still raw from her experience with Carlton. She decided it would be better if Dennis was brought up by his father, who by now had married. As for herself and Lennox, she had big plans to make a new start in America.

'Carlton used to look after Lennox a lot. But I figured that he had a family of his own and I didn't want to break into his family. So I thought it better if I raise him by myself,' she says.

'He was looking after Lennox financially, but he was married and there was nothing he could do for me. I thought it was better to go away and start again somewhere else, and build a better life for me and my son.'

Leaving Dennis with his father and Lennox with Aunt Gee, Violet flew to Chicago, where she had some Jamaican friends. The idea was to find work, set up a home, and send back for her younger son. But she didn't have a visa that would enable her to get a regular job. For over a year she eked out a meagre living picking up a few dollars by working illegally as a childminder and babysitter. She was lonely, dispirited and missing her son when she got an urgent message from her aunt to return home.

'When I got back to London, Aunt Gee was at her wit's end. She was getting on in years by now, and I don't think she could cope with a boisterous, active boy like Lennox. My boys were so different, you see. Dennis was always an easy child. When he was a baby, you could leave him in his crib and as long as he had a bottle he'd be quiet as a mouse. Then when he got older he was always placid and even-tempered.

'Lennox was just the opposite. He was very mischievous. He was a rebel. He liked to fight all the time. If he was playing with other kids he would end up pushing them and wrestling them, and they'd come running to me saying Lennox did this, or Lennox did that, or Lennox was hitting them. When he took up boxing I can't imagine anyone had to teach him how to punch – he's been punching fine since he was a toddler.'

Aunt Gee had her own theory about why Lennox was running wild. 'She blamed the Flintstone's vitamins I used to take. They were chewable things I used to have with orange juice,' say Lennox. 'She said they got me hyper. I was always full of energy, always into something, and fighting would be a reaction. I was never interested in it as a sport – not for a long time. For years all I wanted to be was a fireman.

'I knew my mum had gone away, but I was too young to realize she was in Chicago. I missed her, but she had left me with good people. Auntie Gee was a very nice lady. She was pretty strict. Because I was a hyperactive youngster I was always getting in some sort of mischief, but most times she could handle me.'

Violet came back to take charge. By this time Lennox was going to a primary school off Green Street, not far from Upton Park. 'Lennox was always very lively, but basically he was a very nice boy,' she says. 'The main problem was that he was always so much bigger than children of his own age. Compared to them he was like a giant. If there was a scuffle, he was always so much stronger than they were and they came off second best.

'The thing was that he enjoyed going to school. As I worked mostly nights, I was nearly always there when he came home. He'd bring nearly half the class home for tea every evening. Pure girls – no boys.

'He was a lady's man. He'd say, "Mam, I have seven girlfriends," and bring all seven of them home for tea.'

'One of the most popular games in the school playground was kiss-chase,' says Lennox. 'That's what we used to do all recess. The girls used to like me for some reason. When I was young my complexion was really clear, and people used to say, "Oh, you've got a baby face." I've always liked the company of girls. It's weird – most of my good friends now are girls.'

But then Lennox got himself expelled from primary school. 'I can vividly remember the day it happened,' he says. 'There were two boys playing soccer, and I wanted to join in. I must have been coming up for six then. I was kicking the ball away, and the guy whose ball it was came for it and took it away from me. I said, "No – give me the ball back," and we were in an argument. I just punched him and took the ball.

'Then I got taken to the principal's office, and they left me waiting outside for a long time. I remember all the while I was standing outside I was getting madder and madder. So I punched my hand through the window in the door to the office. I still have the scars – two scars on my right arm – where the glass caught me. I was really mad, and they took me home, bleeding. They sent a note with me saying, "Sorry, but we've had to expel your son for the protection of the other children."'

Violet did not intend to stay in London after her return from Chicago. She had heard from other Jamaican friends that there were good jobs to be had in Kitchener, Ontario, and she decided to emigrate there – this time taking Lennox with her.

She had Lennox's passport picture taken in a photographer's in Bromley-by-Bow, and they both set off for Canada buoyed by the excitement of her son's first trip by plane. It was going to work out this time. Compared to Violet, Mr Micawber was a wet blanket. But there were bad times just around the corner. Her first attempt to give her son a new life in Canada was a failure. Lennox was happy enough there, but he would stay only six months before being sent back to London to begin a five-year separation from Violet.

The so-called friends who offered Violet accommodation charged her an exorbitant rent. Because she was a new arrival in Canada and had not yet paid taxes there, she was obliged to pay for her son's schooling.

'On that first trip to Canada my first impressions were how wide-open and vast it was,' says Lennox. 'When we got off the plane there was snow everywhere. I couldn't believe it. I noticed that people spoke differently, and I liked it because somehow the people seemed to be nicer there.'

He remembers an incident with a red-haired boy at school that sounds like a rerun of the fight between Pip and Herbert Pocket in *Great Expectations*. 'In the recess we used to have toboggan races and snowball fights, and that's all I ever wanted to do,' he says. 'Then one day this red-haired kid said to me, "I hear you're from England and you're pretty tough. Let's have a fight." I didn't want to fight him – I just wanted to play in the snow. But a big circle had formed around us, and he put his fists up and all the other boys were pressing on us to a fight. I went bang, bang, and down he went.

'He got up and said, "Come on, let's go again. I wasn't ready that time." So I knocked him down again. I kept saying I didn't want to fight, and he kept saying he wanted another chance to hit me. Then the bell rang to go back into class and we all walked inside.

'I was dreading the next recess in case he wanted to start all over again. But he came up and said, "Let's play some tobogganing, and snowballs." After that we were good friends. I just wish I could remember what his name was now.'

Though Lennox was content in Canada, his mother was struggling to keep a roof over their heads. There was never enough money to go round. Violet had so little of it that money was all she thought about.

Some days she could just about buy the basics for Lennox but had to go hungry herself.

'It was very difficult. The school fees and the rent were taking nearly every cent I had. There was hardly any money for food, and that's no way to bring up a young, growing boy. After six months it was hopeless. I couldn't see any way out of the mess other than sending Lennox back to London while I worked every hour that God sent to set up a proper home for us. It was a heartbreaking decision, but I had to think what would be better for him in the long run.

'That second parting was really hard – for me and for him. We both cried. Someone I knew was going back to London and they agreed to look after him on the flight for me. I was really low when he walked off through the doors to catch the plane. I explained that he had to go back as things was rough. I said I didn't want him to suffer the way I was suffering, and he understood.

'You hear country-and-western songs about a mother's tears and you think to yourself it's a bit overdone. But that separation was heartbreaking for me. I used to cry all the time. At work they used to call me the weeping willow, because I cried every day. If I was eating a piece of bread, I cried because I didn't know whether my son was eating a piece of bread. I used to worry about Lennox all the time. At first he was staying with Aunt Gee and she was very old by then – she'd long retired. I used to worry whether she was strong enough to look after him properly, and what would happen to him if she got ill.

'It's strange, but those long years of separation created a special bond between us. I would write to him three or four times a week, and I used to get photographs and letters all the time. I phoned him, and now he phones me. We keep in touch all the time. I didn't have any spending money because all my spending money was going on phone bills.'

Back in Britain, Lennox stayed with Aunt Gee for a while. Then he was sent off to boarding-school. But it was hardly *Tom Brown's Schooldays*, the playing-fields of Eton or midnight feasts in the dorm.

Lennox's boisterous conduct, his record of mixing it with the mixed infants, persuaded Aunt Gee that her grand-nephew would be better off in a place where discipline might curb his wild behaviour.

Lennox arrived in the depths of the English countryside – probably Essex, but he doesn't know where exactly – at a place that was not so much a seat of learning as a noisy, friendly, rough-and-tumble mansion where he spent long weeks in order to be kept from under Aunt Gee's feet.

'It was a big house way out in the country run by a couple who were quite well to do. He was a lord-of-the-manor type who had some sort of title,' he says. 'When I arrived, I was the youngest kid there.

'After London I enjoyed the freedom of the countryside. The man was the teacher, and his wife looked after the food for the kids. We all lived together like one big family. We had our lessons together. We played together. There was always something interesting to do. I learned to do woodwork and archery for the first time. They even bought me my own bicycle. It was really good. I've got very happy memories of it.

'They also taught me to write there. I remember writing letters to my mum in Canada. They'd ask me what I wanted to say to her and write it on the blackboard, and I'd copy it down. Each kid had to write so many letters a week.'

He was aware that he had become too much of a handful for his elderly great-aunt. 'There were the usual childhood things like breaking windows with my football,' he says. 'But one time she sent me down to the basement to look for something. I had a candle with me for light. While I was down there it must have caught something on fire as I walked past. I went back upstairs, and she said, "Can't you find it?" When she went downstairs she saw a fire almost starting, and she thought I'd done it on purpose.'

It was in the school in the country that he first found an outlet in sport. 'When I was very young I found I enjoyed the thrill of competition. I think I've always been a competitor, and winning would give me a glow of satisfaction and a good feeling about myself. Even as a little boy I wanted to be first. There was always a bad feeling if I lost, and I didn't like that.

'There was a lot of emphasis on sport and recreation at the school in the country. The guy who looked after the place was a very nice man and he taught me to play ping-pong. I used to spike the ball at him all the time, and he always returned it to me in the same place, helping me get better at ping-pong.

'Then he'd put on the boxing gloves. Nobody out of the kids could fight as well as me. So he would have to put on the boxing gloves with me. I can remember punching away at him, trying to hit him, but never managing to get to him because he was always too big and could keep me at arm's length. It was the first place I put on a pair of boxing gloves.

'I was really happy there, and I enjoyed writing to my mum telling her all about what I was doing. Hidden away somewhere she still must have all the letters I wrote to her, because a couple of years ago I remember her looking through them.'

After an idyllic, carefree year in the country, Lennox was moved back to the East End, to a residential home and school off Romford Road in Forest Gate. 'It wasn't as nice as the other place. There were bigger kids there, and they were rougher,' he says. 'There were more kids, and they'd been sent there for all sorts of reasons – difficult kids, children who weren't wanted, kids who'd got into trouble with the law. It wasn't as nice as the other place, and I didn't like it as much.

'I suppose we were an unruly lot. I remember once we had seen the man in the fish shop picking his nose while he was serving chips one day. So we wrapped up some bangers in a newspaper, lit them, and threw them in his shop.

'There didn't seem to be as many lessons as at the other place. We never really went to school there – we just hung around all day, either watching TV or playing. Half the kids in the place always wanted to escape. In the middle of the night we would sneak out and we were off. Then if you got caught for going out you had to wear shorts all the time instead of long trousers, and you had to go barefoot.

'Other times we would run away and we would ride the Underground trains, up and down, until we were tired. Then we would go up the escalator, find a police station, and they would feed us and bring us back.'

Some weekends and every school holiday Lennox would come out to stay with his brother Dennis and the Daries family in Carpenter's Road, Stratford. 'Everybody was always amazed at how big he was.' Dennis remembers. 'When he was only ten he was wearing size-9 adult shoes. He used to play with kids of my age – much older than he was – but he was always able to stand up for himself. He was tough – a tiger – and he was willing to fight if people pushed him too hard.

'When I was into my teens I started supporting West Ham, and I used to take Lennox along with me to stand on the South Bank at Upton Park. We had a lot of good times and got to know each other much better than when we were smaller. But though we were brothers, and we got along, I wouldn't say we were all that close even then.

'When he went back to Canada, to say I missed him would be untrue. You can't miss somebody you don't really know. You know he's your brother, and you know he's gone elsewhere, but it would be untrue to say I missed him.'

'Dennis's father, Rupert, really liked me a lot,' says Lennox. 'He could deal with me, and I would listen to him. But if he started on Dennis and I'd come in and say, "No, leave him alone," he would leave him alone.

'We used to go down to West Ham baths on Romford Road, where Dennis's dad used to work as a swimming instructor. One day he told Dennis to teach me to swim. Dennis said, "Yes," and pushed me in. I'm there trying to tread water, sinking, and coming up for air. Dennis's dad just reached in, pulled me out, and said, "No, not that way."'

Lennox still didn't like the home off Romford Road. 'I remember I did a lot of kitchen duty, and piles of washing-up,' he says. 'After a few times of running away and having no place to go, it became boring after a while. I think I was maybe in danger of following some of the other kids at that point and getting out of control.

'I remember a kid got me really mad one time. He was bigger than me, and he kept on bugging me. I grabbed a knife from somewhere and I threw it at him. He was standing in a doorway, and the knife stuck in the door jamb right by his head. I told him that's where I'd meant to aim it anyway.

'I never really had a friend in that school. It was like I was all by myself, coping alone. I was put into that place, and I couldn't find one real friend there. Even now if Dennis says to me, "You remember so and so – they were in that school with you," most time I don't know who they are.

'I accepted the fact that my mother was not there. She was in another country a long way away, and I dealt with the case like that. I realized I had a dad, but I wasn't that curious. I knew I had one, because otherwise I would have been a miracle, but the subject wasn't of any big interest to me. I knew my dad was in England, but I had no contact.'

He found solace in sport. 'I've always enjoyed games. I'm a good athlete. I get pleasure from it. But, more than that, sport has been good for me. It's helped me channel my aggression and made me a better person. Early on, even when I was doing sport, I was still kind of hyper to a degree. But in the end it made me think more and use my self-control. Now I am very calm. But if people stroke me the wrong way I can be very vindictive. A lot of people would say that – especially those who know me well. I never forget. I always remember someone who has done something good to me, and I always remember who's done something bad. I hate people having something over on me. I have to get back in some way.

'I think to a degree I had it in me to become a delinquent, but always inside me I was ruled by good ethics and good moral codes. When my mother sent for me to join her in Canada, I think I was caught at the right time. It was a complete change for me, and a change for the better.'

For five years Violet had toiled on the assembly line at the Morval styrofoam factory in Kitchener, packing insulating material. She spent little on herself, saving hard for an apartment big enough for her and Lennox. (She held the same job for seventeen years until Lennox became a professional boxer and he made her stop work.) By 1977 she had set up a place for them on Lancaster Street in Kitchener, and with the help of a Canadian social worker she arranged for Lennox to fly out to join her.

'I tell you, it was a long and hard time for me. All I could think about was getting enough money for an apartment so he could be with me. I just worked and come home and went to work again. I didn't go anywhere. I tell you, for the whole first year nobody even knew I was existing. I'd just go to work and come back home. That's all I did.

'My big outing was going to church. My pastor's wife used to pick me up and take me to church, and we became very good friends. In the end all my prayers were answered – to get enough money, to set up an apartment, and bring him back.

'When I brought him over it was a wonderful feeling. He was due to arrive in Toronto in the afternoon, but I got there in the morning so as to be nice and early.

'I knew it was him as soon as I saw him. He was big, but he'd always been big. I'd watched him growing in the photographs he'd sent me. We'd been apart for years, but we were still very close. I knew exactly what he sounded like from speaking to him so often on the phone, so we didn't really have to get to know each other all over again.

'I kissed him and kissed him. You know what boys are like at twelve – he was the big macho man. He didn't want people to see me kissing him. But I hugged him and kissed him anyway. He just said, "Oh Mam," and looked embarrassed. And I realized that he wasn't a little boy any more.'

'She gave me a kiss that went on so long I didn't think it was ever going to stop,' says Lennox. 'She was overjoyed to see me, because she had missed me so much. I was embarrassed to a certain degree, but I was very happy to see her. When I first came through the gate she was saying in a very loud voice to anyone who would listen to her, "Look, there's my son – there's my son."

'We hadn't met for years, but as soon as I saw her I felt that something that had been missing was suddenly there again. A lost piece of the jigsaw puzzle had fallen back into place.'

2

The First Punch – Whack!

But for a minor skirmish during the First World War, Lennox Lewis would have spent his teenage years living in Berlin.

Kitchener, Ontario, where he grew up and began his boxing career, was by the 1880s Canada's German capital. It began as a settlement of bonneted, black-suited, horse-and-buggy-driving Mennonites, a sect that rejected the worldly values of British North America. The place, built on a cedar swamp, was first known as Sand Hill, then Ebytown, after Bishop Benjamin Eby, who founded the city. But so many German immigrants arrived there in the last three decades of the nineteenth century that the name was changed again – to Berlin. On 9 June 1912, when Berlin celebrated the official proclamation of its cityhood, the ceremony ended with the playing of the dual anthems '*Die Wacht am Rhein*' and 'God Save the King'. Every year the city held a birthday party for the Kaiser, and in the city's main park, in sight of the statue of Queen Victoria, there was a bust of Kaiser Wilhelm II.

When the lights went out in Europe in 1914, the war blew a fuse on the civic harmony of the Berlin 60 miles south-west of Toronto. On the night of 22 August the bust of Kaiser Bill was torn from its plinth and thrown into the Victoria Park lake. It was rescued, and the Kaiser spent the duration hidden in a cupboard in the Concordia Club – a German singing club.

When the bloody war dragged on, blighting hopes that it would all be over by Christmas, Anglo-Canadian patriots campaigned against the teaching of German in public schools and the singing of German songs in the Concordia Club. Most fervently of all, however, they waged a war to change the city's name.

They won. On 1 September 1916 Berlin became Kitchener, after Field Marshal Horatio Herbert ('You Country Needs You') Kitchener, the British secretary for war, who had drowned on 6 June 1916, when the cruiser HMS *Hampshire* struck a mine off the Orkneys.

In a city referendum, 'Kitchener' got 346 votes, the name 'Brock' polled 335 votes, and there were 163 spoiled papers. As a wag at the town meeting said, 'If a skunk lost its stripe no one could think it would smell.'

In 1969, by which time West Germans and Britains had become allies, Kitchener businessmen were emboldened to start North America's first, and only, annual *Oktoberfest*. One of the first public engagement's Lennox Lewis undertook when he returned from Seoul after winning his Olympic gold was to preside over Kitchener's festival of beer, sausage, sauerkraut and oompah music.

When Violet Lewis first arrived in Canada in 1972, Kitchener, with its twin city Waterloo, was an important manufacturing centre in one of Canada's most densely populated areas – making tyres, shoes, buttons, textiles and furniture, as well as packing meat (the best spare-ribs and roasted pig tails in Canada), brewing and distilling.

It was, and remains, clean, neat, and middle-class, with tree-lined streets and shaved grass verges that remind you of so many other trim and respectable North American cities. As the town's historians, John English and Kenneth McLaughlin, say, 'There are no mountain vistas or sweeping river valleys at the pavement's end. Nor are there ethnic neighbourhoods alive with foreign chatter and aromas.'

When Lennox, a gangling, cockney-accented, black twelve-year-old, not averse to using his fists, arrived in Kitchener in 1977, you might expect him to stand out from the crowd. He did. At Elizabeth Ziegler School, his cor-blimey London accent made his mostly white Canadian classmates snigger. Lennox reacted in true East Ender fashion: he thumped them.

'It was the little things that got me started,' says Lennox. 'When I arrived in Kitchener I had a certain saying that kids used in England. Whenever anyone told me to shut up, I'd say, "It's not closing time yet," like I was a store. "When the store's closed, then I'll shut up." It was a stupid little-kid thing, and the other kids used to bug me and mimic me. So I used to go up to them and start a fight.

'They kept on at me about my accent. At one point I felt I was speaking wrong all the time, because anything I said people would always correct me. It put me under quite a lot of stress, and sometimes I felt like not saying anything at all. I'd leave the 't's out of my words and say "wa'er" instead of "water", and they'd bug me about it.

'There was a cycle that kept on repeating itself. They would tease me, I would fight them, and then the headmaster would give me the strap.

'After I had been hauled in front of him three times and he had punished me three times, he said he was getting tired of wasting his energy on me. He told me that if I wanted to fight I ought to be taught how to channel my aggression properly and learn how to box.'

The headmaster had given Lennox the seed of an idea that he would act on a few weeks later. After a dance in Kitchener, Lennox and a pal, Andrew Powis, got involved in some argy-bargy with a group of rival school-dance lotharios. Instead of having a punch-up in the playground, they all agreed to meet up later in the local police gym and settle their argument like gentlemen, with the gloves on. Next evening Andy and Lennox waited outside the gym, but their rivals failed to show up. After half an hour they decided to go in anyway and see what the place looked like.

The Waterloo Regional Police Boxing Association's gym was

presided over by the late Jerome 'Hook' McComb, a craggy sergeant in the local force who was the sort of kind-hearted cop that Pat O'Brien used to play in gangster movies.

For the first two sessions McComb made Lennox and Andrew do a lot of exercises. 'We went down there the next week and it was still the same,' says Lennox. 'I said, "All this exercising is silly. Put me in the ring. I want to box."'

McComb told Lennox to lace on some gloves, and introduced him to Arnie Boehm, who over the next decade was to become his coach, friend and father-figure.

'They didn't have a proper ring. You used to have to box in the circles on the basketball court,' says Lennox. 'So they put me in a circle with one of the guys. The first punch – Whack! I get punched on my nose. I don't like it. My eyes are watering. I think to myself, "This isn't for me." Whack! I get another punch on the nose. "This certainly isn't for me." At the end of that first sparring session I'd half made up my mind that I wasn't going to come back for more. But Arnie persuaded me to give it another go, and as I got better at defending myself I found I wasn't getting hit on the nose at all.'

When a boxing novice gets hit on the nose, automatically his eyes water. He gets flustered, since he thinks that onlookers will assume he is weeping. But then, if he keeps on getting hit on the nose, by the end of his first public round he probably will be weeping. 'Lennox was no different from any other boy,' says Arnie. 'He didn't quite cry, but at the end of the round his eyes sure were watering.'

Arnie Boehm (pronounced 'Beam'), who is now sixty, was a power-line man with the local hydroelectric company. His and his wife Verna's five children were grown up and leaving home. He had time on his hands, which he spent helping out Hook McComb down at the gym. He is a tough, wiry man with a Zapata-moustache, who jokes about his own amateur boxing career, fighting through his youth at between 139 and 165 lb. 'I had fifty fights and won all but forty-nine of them.' He is putting himself down. He can't have been that bad, since he won half his fights. 'I was no great shakes as a boxer,' he says, 'but I've got the knack of coaching others.'

Today the Kitchener police gym is much as it was then — a cavernous basketball court, with notices that warn against the wearing of street shoes, and the forbidding air of a place that has witnessed the shedding of sweat, blood, and tears. To gain admittance must have been daunting for a twelve-year-old-boy. The gym is behind the police station, and to get in you have to get past the desk sergeant. If your name checks out on his list, the gun-toting cop unlocks a door and you are ushered up to the gym by the stairs beyond the cells and the squad room. Sometimes above the scuff of rubber on the gym floor you can hear the sound of cops firing their police magnums in the shooting-gallery out the back.

'I'd seen Lennox come in. He was with a friend of his called Andy,' says Arnie. 'You could see that they were both a bit nervous, but at the same time there was an eagerness about them. They were clowning and joking, pushing each other, giggling and hee-heeing as boys will do in a boxing gym.

'At my first coaching session I began as I usually do by asking them what their interests were in the gym. They both said they wanted to learn to box. So I told them to turn up regularly, be prepared to work, but don't expect miracles. "I can show you a thousand things," I said, "but I can't do one thing for you. In a boxing bout you're on your own. The coach can't get in there with you and help you out."

'A boxer has got to learn the lesson of self-reliance. That's why I let beginners have a bang at each other early on. If a boy gets hurt and he says, "That's enough," he's never going to make a boxer. The thing with Lennox was, sure his eyes watered, but he thought, "Whoa, I've got to do something about this," and he fought back. He had heart.'

His mother wasn't wholly in favour of the new hobby. 'I didn't want him to get hurt. I told him if he wanted to do sport, why didn't he concentrate on basketball?' she says. But by then it was too late — Lennox was already hooked on boxing. 'She did object at first. But when she saw how good I was at boxing she didn't mind so much,' says Lennox. 'I suppose if I had come home with a broken nose or a thick lip every time it might have been a different story, but she knew that I could take care of myself.'

Violet was also highly suspicious about her boy's middle-aged friend at the gym, Arnie Boehm. 'I was worried about this guy Arnie, because it was "Arnie this" and "Arnie that". He was staying out late, and Arnie was driving him home. And I was kind of wondering about him because you hear stories about guys in gyms and young boys, and I didn't even known whether or not this Arnie was married. Lennox was telling me, "He's a good guy, Mum," but I still made him bring him home so that I could have a good look at him. And like Lennox said, Arnie's a good guy.'

Taking up boxing didn't mean that Lennox planned to drop other sports. From now on, though, he used them as a means of getting fitter for his boxing. 'I enjoy team games, but I told my mum that I could just as easily get hurt on the basketball court or playing American football,' he says. 'And, anyway, I'd already got used to winning trophies. In a team game you have to wait until the end of the season to pick up a cup or a shield. But, in boxing, every time I fought in a competition I picked up a trophy. And I didn't have to share it with the rest of the squad – it was all mine.'

Roadwork, physical training and combative sparring sessions became a daily ritual for the young boy. 'Even when I was showing Lennox the basics I could see that he had a great natural talent for the sport,' says Arnie. 'Ninety per cent of your defence is in your stance – the way you hold your hands and position your body, where you place your feet and put your chin. He did things naturally, almost without being shown what to do.

'He was such a good pupil, and so eager to learn. He was interested to the point where he would look me straight in the eye and hang on to every word I said, eager to take in the next bit of advice. He was the most attentive pupil I've ever had. A lot of my kids who aspired to be boxers would talk while I was talking, or look around or fool around. But he always looked me straight in the eye, hungry for what I had to tell him.

'In those early days Lennox, Andy and another young guy called Adam Hanson used to spar together a lot. They had wars, and I would let them go for as long as nobody got hurt. I supervised it carefully, but I let them belt away at each other to see who had the heart, who had the desire. They were good boys. Now he's world champion Lennox can thank Adam and Andy for all that early sparring they did with him.'

It was Arnie who bought Lennox his first boxing gear — just as it was Arnie who fed the growing teenager extra meals, slipped him pocket money, taught him to drive, to fish, to make cement, to fix a fuse, explained the facts of life, remembered his birthdays, teased him if he got above himself, encouraged him about his schoolwork, and did all the many little things a father does for a son he loves.

'We started out just as boxer and coach in the gym, but that blossomed out into a kind of father-and-son relationship. Some of my best impressions of him were not of his accomplishments in the ring so much as of his development as a boy. He had some preconceived notions. From the start I realized he needed some fatherly direction, guidance, discipline, or whatever it is a boy looks for in a father.

'He had a terrible inferiority complex when I first met him. He was a basket case when he first came here as far as I was concerned. He was so introverted and so untrusting of virtually everyone. It took him a while to be comfortable with grown-ups.

'We just hit it off. It was as though fate had directed us towards each other. I had just finished raising a family of my own, and I was proud of their development. I liked what I saw in Lennox. I felt I knew what he needed, and I tried to provide it for him.

'More than just boxing, I wanted to give him the things I thought he should have in life. I wanted to teach him about the outdoors. I wanted to teach him about dealing with other people — both male and female. About his health, about money, work – even religion. I didn't impose anything on him – I just tried to guide him and set an example.'

When Lennox was twelve he was close to 6 feet tall, and his shoe size was creeping up to 12. (It is now 15½.) 'At that age he was not a frail boy by any stretch of the imagination,' says Arnie. 'But he wasn't very muscular, and he looked a bit like a plant that was growing too quickly for its own good. One day I was showing him how important it is to trim your toenails properly – like I had with my own sons – and he was very concerned about his big feet. We used to have to go and get his feet measured and have special shoes made, and that was an embarrassment for him. I'd say, "Don't worry about it. Some day the rest of your body will catch up to your feet and you'll be a hell of a big man. If you want to grow an oak tree, you've got to have a good base.' And that would reassure him. In many ways he was a gawky, self-conscious ugly duckling, but he's grown up into a heck of a nice fellow.

'I bought him so much stuff over the years. Baseball boots. I bought him his first jockstrap. A dentist friend of mine fixed him a special gum-shield.

The dentist wears a T-shirt which proclaims, "The only man in Canada who frightens Lennox Lewis." But I did it all for my own, and I've done it for other kids too since. I figured it was a better investment than spending it on booze and a lot of women.'

With his mix of sentimentality, beguiling toughness and gritty advocacy of simple male values, Arnie looks like a bit-part player who specializes in tough cavalry sergeants. Under 'religion', Arnie could put down two entries: Roman Catholic and recovering alcoholic. He once took Lennox to midnight mass. 'There were hundreds of people there, and Lennox looked around and whispered to me, "Have you noticed I'm the only black person in this place?" He was right. But I said to him, "No you're not. Both of us are." '

It was odd how many people in the preparation of this book said of

Lennox, 'I was a father to him.' But Arnie really was, and there is no doubting his love for the young man he first met in Kitchener's stark police gym sixteen years ago.

'He was a good boy. It was a lot of pleasure to do stuff with him – shopping or camping, whatever we did. I have pictures of him sitting by the camp-fire. He loves the outdoors, and he's sitting by a camp-fire singing like a bird.'

For his part, Lennox looks on Arnie as a stand-in father. 'I think he felt I needed the guidance of a man as I was growing up,' he says. 'He looked at the situation of my mother being on her own, and where I was coming from, and decided to be there for me. We just took to each other straight away. He became a father-figure not only to me but to a whole bunch of us. He's just that way. He's a very nice man. He bought me a whole lot of things he couldn't really afford to buy me – my first headgear and mouthpiece. He would take me camping, show me how to fix things, drive me home. He showed real care.

'He was an important source of advice when I was growing up. Until I filled out I really was self-conscious about my height and the size of my feet. Kids used to ask me how big my feet were. "Big enough to fit into your mouth," I'd say. They'd tell me my feet looked like boats. I'd snap right back at them, "And they're going to sail right into your face." He told me not to mind all that stuff – that one day people wouldn't poke fun at me.

'His only really big failure with me was fishing. For years he tried to get me interested in angling. He'd take me out and we'd sit on the river-bank for hours, and all I'd do was go to sleep. I used to hate baiting the hooks. I could never pick up a live worm and put it on my hook, because I didn't like the way they wriggled round and the squirminess of them. So I used to kill mine first and put them on the hook when they'd stopped wriggling.

'My other great memory of Arnie is him teaching me to drive. I had my lesson in an automatic car, and I thought it was a breeze. But the first car I got had a shift stick, and I didn't know how to operate it. I had to get Arnie to give me a quick lesson so I could drive it off the car lot. He's never let me forget it.'

In his first official amateur bout, Lennox knocked out Junior Lindsay in two rounds. He then went undefeated for three years, and proved so good as a boy boxer that he soon began to run out of opponents. No one of his own age was big enough or good enough to fight him. By the time he was fifteen and Ontario Golden Gloves champion he had run out of opposition in his weight class – 165 lb.

On 28 October 1980 – just fifty-six days after his fifteenth birthday, he took on twenty-two-year-old, Kingsley Hataway of Toronto and scored a points decision over the former Canadian amateur middleweight champion. With the lack of competition in the junior division, he was forced to move up to look for challengers in the senior open class.

His first defeat came at the hands of Donovan 'Razor' Ruddock when Ruddock was eighteen and Lennox only fifteen. 'The boy wasn't even shaving yet, and Razor was a grown man,' says Arnie. 'Ruddock just nicked it on points. Lennox gave as good as he got, but tired in the last round because compared to the other guy he was still only a baby.'

'Later on, when he became a professional, Razor used to boast how he'd sparred with me in Kitchener,' says Lennox. 'He'd brag about how he'd spilled my blood all over my shoes, and my blood was all over the gym floor. But it was only age that gave him the edge, and then only for a while, because he was stronger than me. I always thought that 3–2 decision against me was dubious. It was a selection bout to decide who to send down to fight in a tournament against an American team, and they wanted older boys in the team. Razor was older than me, so he was given the decision.'

At home his mother had given him the nickname Junior. The name stuck so well that people assumed that that was his given name and they began calling him Junior on the register at Margaret Avenue School, where he was now a pupil. He carried the name all through his teens, reverting to Lennox at around the age of seventeen. As his mum says, 'It got to be ridiculous. There he would be towering over me and I'd be calling him Junior. The name didn't fit any more, so I started calling him Lennox or Lennie.'

Lennox stopped counting how many amateur bouts he'd boxed long before the 1988 Olympics, but he was never floored in around 104 contests. He had about 95 wins — 52 by stoppage — and lost only 9 times. He learned from every defeat, and the next time he faced an opponent who had previously beaten him he invariably won.

One of those defeats was in the Canadian Intermediate Champion-ships in 1982, when Lennox was seventeen. He had just dropped the name Junior. 'I was always for changing his name back to what it really was,' says Arnie. 'I told him, "You're too big to be still called Junior. Lennox sounds so much more impressive. It suits you. Just think — 'Lethal Lennox Lewis' — that's pretty good." So we got a robe made with "Lethal Lennox" embroidered on the back.'

But Lethal Lennox didn't live up to his new ring name. 'Would you believe it? He goes and gets beaten by Hughie Thompson,' said Arnie. 'The story behind that was unbelievable. I knew some people in Niagara Falls and asked them if ever they went across the border into the States to look out for a pair of boxing boots — size 14. Pick them up for Lennox and I'd repay them.

'Well, a pal of mine — Gene Somerville — said he'd got them for me, and I went down to collect them. They seemed fine, but they had brand-new shiny leather soles. They were the kind that old-timers like me used to wear — the ones you had to rub in rosin to get a grip on the canvas.

'Lennox had never worn real boxing boots before — only trainers — so he was all proud in his new boots. And what have they got for a canvas? — slippery vinyl surface! He's boxing a guy who has no right to be in the ring with him, but Lennox is slipping and sliding all over the place. He can't get any leverage for his punches, because his feet keep sliding from under him. I couldn't take the boots off between rounds and say, "Box barefoot," so he hardly laid a glove on the other guy and lost the fight. I bet Hughie Thompson is telling people to this day he beat Lennox Lewis. But he didn't beat Lennox – it was those lousy boots that beat us.'

3

Bigger Things to Come

Training for boxing is a monotonous, masochistic ritual. If you want to be a champion you cannot shirk the sweaty daily routine of running, brutal exercise sessions and punishing workouts in the gym. There are few sports which make such physical demands on a competitor as boxing does. The Roman philosopher and playwright Seneca wrote of boxers, 'Their very training involves pain.'

There is an oft-repeated cliché intoned by gnarled old trainers in countless gyms, who mutter it without for a moment realizing the provenance of the saying. 'No pain, no gain,' they say – echoing Adlai Stevenson's acceptance speech at the 1952 Democratic Convention.

For a youngster who takes the decision that this is the sport for him, it will take some eight years before he can expect to be even approaching his peak as an international amateur or a ranked professional.

As well as a high degree of technical skill and natural ability, a good boxer needs to improve the speed of his foot and hand movements, his endurance, his strength and his joint flexibility – particularly at the hip and shoulder.

The need for supreme fitness is obvious. In football or rugby, if a man is below par he can rely on his team-mates to cover for him, or the coach pulls him off the pitch. If you have an off day in boxing there are no substitutes – there is just you and your opponent in a ring, and there is nowhere to hide. As Randall 'Tex' Cobb, the American heavyweight who lost a brutally one-sided title fight with Larry Holmes, has said, 'If you screw up in tennis it's 15–0. If you screw up in boxing it's your ass.'

Ever since he took up the sport, Lennox has been a diligent, vigorous trainer. 'I predicted Lennox would be world champion in 1981, when he was sixteen. The next year, even though he lost in the final of the Canadian Nationals, I convinced Lennox that he could be a world-beater,' says Arnie Boehm.

'I said, "It's going to require dedication. Day in day out of hard work." He accepted that, and he applied himself. When he was a boy in Canada you could hear the armchair quarterbacks saying that he didn't have the killer instinct, he lacked the will, he didn't have the courage. The people who say that don't know Lennox.

'The key to this man is that he doesn't like to be beaten at anything. If you beat him at tiddleywinks he'll go away and practise all night, then the next day he'll come back and beat you ten times in a row. That's the sort of guy he is. He doesn't like to come second at anything.'

When he was a boy, Lennox used to get up early and run through the empty streets. The residential districts of Kitchener, neat and respectable, are the fulfilment of every immigrant's dream – trim lawns, two cars in most driveways, and a basketball hoop over every garage door.

If it was raining he used to test his reactions by throwing punches at the raindrops as they dripped from the branches of trees. Drip, jab. Drip, hook. Drip, jab.

In winter he would stride out through the virgin snow, taking his longest steps – imagining that kids when they woke might think the footprints had been left there by the Big Friendly Giant or by some alien who had rampaged that way overnight.

The loneliness of the long-distance runner creates a dreamlike state. While pounding along mile after mile, the drug of running opens up a vast prairie of the imagination.

'Your mind zooms all over the place,' says Lennox. 'Obviously you're thinking about your pace. Or, if you're running with someone, how you're going compared to them. But on a long run the strangest thoughts can come into your head. You'll get into a rhythm and suddenly a song you thought you'd long forgotten will come back crystal-clear from some corner of your mind.

'When I was a kid and I was running I would sometimes fantasize about boxing. Kids go through that big fantasy thing – pretending they're a pop star with a Fender guitar, or being one of the cool guys in the movies. I'd think about boxing. But in an odd way I was never Muhammad Ali – it was always *me* fighting his fights. On those runs I must have knocked out George Foreman a hundred times in my imagination. But it was always me doing it my way, never Ali doing it his.

'I train hard now, because that's my job. Bankers go to the bank. Welders go to the metalwork shop. Boxers do their road work and go to the gym. We're all professionals. We work hard all the time at what we get paid for. But in my teens I can't really say I worked that hard to get fit. To me it was all sort of being a kid at school doing a whole load of sport I enjoyed. It was like a circular thing – my basketball got me fit for my football, and the football got me fit for my boxing, and the boxing got me tuned up for track and field. It was like all the energy I'd misused earlier was being channelled into sport.'

The first major international title Lennox won, in November 1983, was the gold medal in the World Junior Championships at Santo Domingo in the Dominican Republic. 'I convinced him that he could win it, and he trained for that title like someone possessed,' says Arnie. 'I'd take him to the Centennial Stadium in Kitchener and it would be freezing rain. I'd be in a snow suit and his girlfriend at the time, Bernita Drenth, would be all wrapped up in scarves and water-proofs and he'd be out there braving the elements for hours on end.

'One of the goals we set him was to get fit by running up and down the bleachers in the stadium. In freezing rain it was not the safest way to train, but it was an excellent method of developing explosive power. I told him that when he could run up and down twenty-five times non-stop he would be ready.

'A few days before we left to go to Santo Domingo, he said he was going to do the twenty-five, to go for it. I counted. Twenty-five times he did it. We all cheered. He said, "One more." Then another. He did it twenty-seven times, and we were all cheering like mad.'

'It was straight out of the *Rocky* movies. I could hear the music from the film going in my head, and it gave me a kind of power,' says Lennox. 'It was like Sylvester Stallone running up the stone steps of that building, only I was running up and down the bleachers. The music from the film was so clear in my head it was like I had a Walkman on. And when I'd done the twenty-seven it was just like a still from the movie – I was at the top of the stadium arms aloft, and all three of us were cheering.'

The strict training paid off. In front of 8,000 cheering enthusiasts at El Palacio de los Deportes in Santo Domingo, Lennox had to fight in temperatures approaching 90 degrees to win his first-ever gold medal, but he was never in trouble.

Victory, though, was hollow – a foretaste of how he would win his WBC title. His scheduled opponent in the final, the Cuban Pedro Nemicio had broken a bone in his right hand during his semi-final, giving Lennox a walk-over to win his medal.

The manner in which he bulldozed his way to the last stage was spectacular, however, and the Cuban coach sportingly assured him that he would probably have beaten his man anyway. Against the highly rated Vincent Jones of the USA, Lennox came out quickly and knocked his man down in the first round. Jones took a standing count in the second, and was hopelessly outclassed in the third. All five judges gave Lewis the decision.

In his semifinal bout Lewis knocked over the Romanian, Durin, in round one, forced him to take a standing count of eight in the second, and toyed with him in the third.

Lennox liked his first taste of the big time. Confident of his ability,

Boehm moved him up to senior level, two years before he needed to. In January 1984 he won his first senior international bout with a 5–0 verdict over Bengt Cederquist of Sweden in Stockholm and returned home to be named Canada's under-twenty male athlete of the year.

'It was a good few months,' recalls Lennox, 'It was a big disappointment when the Cuban was declared unfit in Santo Domingo, because I wanted the thrill of the battle. But that didn't take away the huge elation I felt at winning my first gold. It also helped underline the importance of hard training. You only get out what you put in. I'd done all the work and got the reward for it. I was in perfect condition. The heat didn't bother me at all. At the end of my two fights I wasn't even breathing hard.'

For a big man, Lennox has the athleticism and mobility of a welter- or middleweight. When he runs, his speed belies his size. He can do a mile in 6 minutes 30 seconds and 100 metres in 13 seconds. In his high-school grid-football team he was a star running-back, and at basketball he was a high-scoring forward. He was approached by talent scouts wanting him to take both sports further, but he was too busy with his boxing.

'I think he could have been good at any sport he tried his hand at,' says Arnie. 'When he was at high school, Cameron Heights, the coach, Ron Bell, wanted to put him in some track and field events. So they put him in the shot-put, and he wins that straight off. Then they asked him to have a go at the javelin, and the very first time he threw one he broke the school's javelin record.

'He's a natural athlete. But boxing is what he's built for. His size, desire, genes, what have you, make him the perfect super-heavyweight. Big guys are a dime a dozen – there are lots of big guys. But big guys with a little bit of ambition, they are fewer. And brains, they are fewer still. One with ability, brains, ambition and heart – that's priceless. To get all those qualities in one guy makes him one in a million.'

Courtney Shand, Lewis's strength-and-fitness conditioner, is a graduate in physical-training studies at Fanshawe College, Ontario. He looks like an earnest, unsmiling preacher, with the basilisk gaze of Sonny Liston, but when you get to know him he is warm and generous – one of the nicest guys in the training camp. His job is to monitor the boxer's fitness and act as goad and encourager to Lennox while he trains.

They were exact contemporaries at Cameron Heights High School. 'Lennox has always been in tremendous physical condition,' says Courtney. 'In football he was like a secret weapon for us. Every time he was tackled he would throw himself forward, and because he was so tall, we'd gain an extra two yards.'

'He's always been very competitive, and I remember his mum telling me that when he was a young kid he used to sit up at night and watch people doing things – playing cards, or games, or mending things. Then the day after he'd be able to do it. And then the day after that he'd be able to do it even better than the person he'd been watching.

'The thing I've always admired about him is that he's very strong mentally. He knows exactly what he wants, and he knows exactly how he's going to get it. In our last year at college we played in a football final against Eastwood Collegiate. We'd beaten them earlier in the season, but in that final they murdered us. They beat us 21–1, and they only gave us that one point so that they could get a field position.

'There were a lot of us graduating that year, so it was our last game as a team. On the bus coming back, everybody had their heads down and most of us were crying. Lennox and I were sitting together and I had my head down, crying. I looked up, and Lennox was the only one on the bus sitting up and not shedding a tear. I said to him, "Don't you feel bad that we lost?" He said, "I'm not going to cry – I've got bigger things to come. There's a lot more for me to achieve in life than this little high-school championship."

'That's always stuck in my mind. There was no way he was being arrogant. He was so totally certain that he was going to do something big with his life.'

Yet Lennox insists that even then he still hadn't yet committed himself to a career as a professional boxer. 'At Santo Domingo I thought I must be pretty good to do so well. But boxing was still only a sport to me, and I didn't think of it as a way of earning my living.

'It was only at the 1984 Olympics it suddenly began to dawn on me that maybe I'd make it as a pro. In Los Angeles I was up against more mature boxers who had much more experience than I did, yet I could match them in skill, and in some departments I was even better than they were.

'But when I was at college I was like all the other college boys. Sport was a hobby. Boxing was just my way of having fun.'

4

Come on, Chicken – Hit Me

In the eyes of decent folks, inmate number 922335 incarcerated in the Indiana Youth Prison in Plainfield, Indiana, is a bully and rapist – a delinquent from the Brownsville ghetto who made millions of dollars with his fists and then spiralled out of control, his ring career destroyed by his conviction for raping beauty queen Desiree Washington. But Lennox Lewis remembers Mike Tyson as the buddy he sparred with in the spring of 1984. 'When I met him he was a pleasant, almost shy, kind of guy and we got on well,' says Lennox. 'I don't know how much he's changed over the years, but I'm not convinced he's the big ogre people paint him.'

In the April of the Los Angeles Olympics year, Lennox and coach Arnie Boehm arrived at the end of a dirt road in Catskill, upstate New York. They'd come to the big, white-painted nineteenth-century house where Tyson lived with his mentor and legal guardian Cus D'Amato and his trainer Kevin Rooney on a bluff overlooking the Hudson River.

Lennox was to spend eight days there, in the training camp with Tyson, running up the forested mountains, competing to see who could do the most push-ups or bench presses, and sparring together in the gym over the fire station on Catskill's main street. Lennox was eighteen; Tyson, a few months younger, seventeen.

They lived in the fourteen-roomed house as part of the boxing family. Camille Ewald, the amiable woman who owned the place and had taken D'Amato in, did the cooking. Meals were taken together and, while they ate, D'Amato — reader of Thoreau, fisherman, amateur astronomer, luminary, sage and Maharishi of the ring — would give them the benefit of his vast boxing knowledge.

D'Amato believed there was more to creating a champion than simply honing his ring-craft or building up strength and endurance. A true champion had a philosophy, an attitude, a focused idea of his destiny.

Some people dismissed his notions as a lot of pretentious flap-doodle, but there is a core of cracker-barrel wisdom to them. Bronx-born D'Amato died at the age of seventy-seven in 1985, but his sayings are still a part of boxing lore. Like a doorstep missionary, he was a great one for improving tracts. You can find them thumbtacked to the walls of gyms everywhere:

Boxing is a contest of will and skill, with the will generally overcoming the skill, unless the skill of one man is much greater than the skill of the other.

As they sweat through exercises, their daily regime of Stakhanovite punishments, boxers the world over are likely to be stared at by his baleful texts:

Fear is like a fire. If you control it, as we do when we heat our houses, it is a friend. When you don't, it consumes you and everything you do and everything around you.

There were some great conversations around that table. For someone like Lennox, whose world was already boxing, it was like sitting at the feet of a guru,' says Arnie Boehm.

'Around that time Lennox and I would go to Toronto to spar with Razor Ruddock quite often — twice a week if possible. A lot of times Razor would give some sort of silly excuse and say, "I can't spar tonight — I've got a pimple on my bum," or whatever. So I came home one evening when he'd done that to us and got a telephone call: "This is Cus D'Amato." I said, "*The* Cus D'Amato?" "Yes, this is so."

'He said he'd heard I'd got a promising young heavyweight, and propositioned that we fly down there for a week or ten days to work out with a young man he had called Mike Tyson.

'I told him that would be great. But I wondered how he knew my name. He said to me, "Do you know a boxer called Razor Ruddock?" I said, "Yeah. We should have sparred with him today, but he didn't turn up." He said, "The same thing happened here. Razor came down here, took one look at Mike, and didn't even unpack his bags."

'That time in Catskill was like an intensive study course on boxing, with lectures and practicals from the resident guru. I learned a lot in the sparring, and picked up some interesting ideas from Cus D'Amato,' says Lennox. 'Today Tyson's got that very tough image. The first impression I got too was that he was a hard case. He was short, muscular and rough-looking – just like he is now. But what surprised me most of all was his voice. It was a very light, high voice, and when he spoke it was almost like a squeak.

'We made an odd sort of pair, because at the time I was skinny and lanky and he was stocky and quite small. But we got on fine.'

Lennox had a cold when he got there, and Arnie was concerned about him sparring with Tyson. 'The two boys got on fine,' says Arnie. 'They were running together, training and joking, like two old friends. On day three Cus said, "Do you think we could spar today?" Lennox had a bit of a cold – he wasn't 100 per cent – but he said he wanted to go ahead and spar.

'So the guys get ready. We lace the gloves on them. They're joking and the best of pals. Cus rings the bell and Tyson comes tearing across the ring like a raging tiger. He caught Lennox completely by surprise and he put quite a number on Lennox, just for a few seconds. So Lennox's nose is bleeding – partly from a cold he had, but mostly from Tyson's onslaught.

'So at the end of the round I'm wiping him down and whispering in his ear, "You know we don't have to spar today. We can spar again tomorrow." Lennox said, "No, I know what to do now." I told him OK, but if it got rough like that again I would stop it.

'So the second round starts and Lennox is boxing well – sticking and moving. In fact sometimes he'd even dodge and run to get away from Mike, because he wasn't accustomed to meeting a guy that ferocious. So the first day it was all Mike.

'The second day things started to even up. Lennox was evading his charges and getting in good punches of his own. The third day? Outright war. Lennox was giving as good as he got, and a bit more. Tyson got so frustrated at one point he said, "Come on, come on, chicken – hit me." And bang – Lennox nailed him.

'Then Cus stopped it and said, "That's enough of that. I don't want any more of that showboating." That's the kind of fatherly control Cus had over Mike. But the sparring was fine after that. They boxed. They sparred. They tried to knock the hell out of each other. At the end of the week of non-stop battle Lennox had learned so much. And if you had to score how it went, you'd be hard put to the name the winner. I tell you, it was very close. If ever they met in a real match it would be one hell of a fight.

'Neither boy wanted to lose face. Tyson would come charging in, and Lennox certainly wouldn't back down. He'd take a step to the side or sway out of range, and then he'd throw some big punches of his own. He had Mike under control by the end of the week, and Mike was getting more and more riled.

'It was ferocious. But after sparring, immediately they got out of the ring, they'd be laughing and carrying on again just like nothing had happened. That's the way Mike is. Inside the ring he's hostile, ready to destroy you. Outside it he's a nice, friendly guy.

'The image of boxers to some people is that they are thick, that they fight because they can't do anything else. But Lennox is no fool, and neither is Tyson. Mike's a very intelligent person. A lot of the put-downs are simple jealousy on the part of wanabees. Sure, Mike is a rough-looking guy, and he talks tough. A lot of people object to that. But there's a softer side to him if you're around him for a while.'

'That first day in the ring he was throwing punches like he wanted to take my head off,' says Lennox. 'After a while I put on my Muhammed Ali routine for him. I started dancing around the ring, and every time he got close to me I held him and closed him down. He was very strong and busy, but I didn't ever think he'd become world champion. What pissed me off about him was that he was so strong yet he was younger than I was.

'What annoyed him most was I wouldn't stand there and get hit. When a man's trying to hit you, you've got to use up the whole ring. I was dancing like Ali. He couldn't catch me, and it made him angry as hell.

'He kept pigeons, and he showed me his lofts. He was really quite an expert, and gentle with the pigeons in a way you'd never guess by looking at him. Apart from pigeons and boxing, his other great interest was girls. I remember he kept phoning this girl from Montreal. I met her a year ago and she said, "Hiya – remember me? I'm the girl Mike Tyson used to ring from the Catskills." And I said, "Oh, *you're* that girl." Tyson kept on at me asking me if I knew this girl in Montreal, as though I knew every girl in Canada, and I'd say to him, "No, Mike – no I don't."

'But he kept on phoning her, and Cus was always complaining about the phone bills. He would just spend hours on the phone, phoning girls all over the place. He would send roses and candy and everything. When I met up with this girl in Montreal she said that's how he was with girls.

'I thought at one time that it was ordained that Tyson and I would fight each other as professionals. Cus D'Amato kept saying, "You two will meet again in the ring one day." I didn't believe him and said, "Oh yeah?" But over the years I came round to thinking that it could happen. If it did, it would certainly be a good fight. But in the light of where Mike is, and what my plans are, I don't see myself still being in the sport when he comes out of prison.'

At the Catskill hideaway they had one of the largest collections of old fight films in the world. They belonged to Jim Jacobs, co-manager of Tyson, who was D'Amato's backer. A one-time sales manager of a business-machines company and a national handball champion, Jacob's hobby was collecting boxing films and newsreels. He had five thousand vintage fight movies from the era 1894 to 1953. In the evenings, after training, Tyson and D'Amato would ask their guests to nominate which champion they wanted to see that night.

'For anyone interested in boxing it was like a national archive. Mike would hang up an old sheet and set up the projector and you could call up any of the champions – Dempsey, or Louis. Mike Tyson is like a walking encyclopaedia of boxing history, so I learned a lot from him that week. We could pick up on all the moves and bits of know-how from the great fighters on the screen,' says Lennox.

One night when Lennox had turned in to bed early, Arnie sat with Tyson watching classic fights. 'I'd asked to see the second Ezzard Charles–Jersey Joe Walcott fight. (Charles won on points over fifteen rounds in Detroit.) We watched the fight, and as Mike was putting away the projector I sat chatting to him.

'I said, "You know, Mike, you've got it made. You've got Cus – a guy who cares about you – you've got a nice place to live, and all the ability you could ask for. Some day you'll likely be champion of the world. You're going to have all kinds of money. And just think of all the cars and the girls." He said, "Wait a minute. Give all that money and all those cars and girls to somebody else. Just give me a good fight." That's true. I think the ring is where he feels most fulfilled. Now he's in prison and can't fight any more, I guess he's missing the thing he enjoys most.

'If Lennox and Mike ever got to box again – in public next time – it would be a battle and a half. The fans would love to see it, I'd certainly love to see it, and it would make a fortune for both of them.

But I don't think it'll happen. If Mike still wants to fight when he gets out of prison he'll never quite be the force he was. The years in prison will have broken his momentum. It'll be hard for him to get back again to the greatness he had. And, by the time he comes out of jail, Lennox will almost certainly be involved in a whole new brilliant career doing something else.'

The two boxers did not meet up again at the Los Angeles Olympics. Tyson lost his berth in the American team to Henry Tillman, and, claiming he was a victim of amateur boxing politics, turned pro. He earned $500 for his first fight, in March 1985, when he demolished Marvis Frasier (the son of 'Smokin' Joe' Frasier) within the echo of the first bell.

Also missing from California were the Soviets, Cuba and most of the Eastern-bloc countries. As a tit-for-tat for the Moscow boycott four years earlier, they all stayed at home. This diluted the boxing competition, since it meant that Cuba's veteran three-time gold-medallist Teofilio Stevenson was absent, as was the rated Soviet super-heavyweight Alexander Yagubkin.

The American approach to staging their third Olympic Games was to make it bigger and noisier than ever before. They wanted to make the previous show, put on in Moscow, look pale by comparison. The result was one of the most garish games ever, in which the sport was all but engulfed in a luminous tidal wave of schmaltz. At the opening ceremony a thousand-voiced choir sang; a marching band of eight hundred musicians strutted their way into the amphitheatre; a man with a jet-pack flew through the California smog to land on the track; and eighty-four white baby-grand pianos played Cole Porter. For those who'd been waiting for Olympic Games opening ceremonies to hit rock bottom, the suspense was over.

Lennox tuned up for the biggest competition in his life by spending two weeks in a conditioning camp in Kelowna, British Columbia, late in June. He ran, did route marches across country, and impressed national boxing coach Taylor Gordon by finishing second in a

12-mile run on the final day. Long-distance runners are usually spar-sely built, and for a big man to do so well in a near half-marathon showed how fit he was.

'When Lennox returned from BC he was in marvellous shape. By that time – coming up to his nineteenth birthday – he was a solid 215 lb. It was all muscle – no fat at all. If he'd wanted to take any weight off he'd have to have done it with a rasp,' says Arnie Boehm. 'I was holding the heavy bag for him one night when he came back, and he was hurting me right through the bag.'

With the field thinned by the boycott, some experts reckoned that Lennox could be the giant-killer of the super-heavy division. But the world amateur champion Tyrrell Biggs, with only six losses in 109 bouts, was the obvious favourite, with Italy's Francesco Damiani as the main danger.

Before getting into the ring, Lennox had an unofficial bout in the Canadian team's quarters. His opponent was the sprinter Ben Johnson, who four years later would win the Seoul 100 metres only to be disgraced and lose his medal in a drugs scandal.

'I was always hanging out with the track team at Los Angeles. Some of the guys were friends of mine, and I knew some of the girls in the relay team,' says Lennox. 'I came down from my room and I was playing pool with the track guys. Someone noticed that Ben Johnson had left his dog-tags behind. Security was very tight, and you couldn't go anywhere without your dog-tags, so when I'd finished my game of pool I said, "I'm going upstairs. I'll give them to him." I grabbed his identification, went upstairs, and was looking for him. I couldn't see him, so I chatted to a few of my friends and came downstairs to play pool again. I told everybody, "If you see Ben, tell him I've got his dog-tags."

'I'm playing pool, and suddenly this guy comes up behind me and tries to grab my dog-tags. And it was Ben. He was very upset. He thought I had taken his identification stuff on purpose. He was really wild. He took off his Walkman and shaped up like he wanted to fight me.

45

'I'm saying, "What's going on?" And he's talking so fast I can't understand him. There was some pushing, and he grabbed my shirt and ripped it. Then he ran at me and butted me in the chest. So I just grabbed his head and both arms and squeezed and squeezed until he said, "OK, OK."

'I was very upset, went up to my dormitory, and locked myself in. Later I heard a whole lot of banging on my door. I think it was a crowd of the track team coming up to fight me. But nothing happened, and it all quietened down eventually. Next day I noticed that when he was out on the track getting ready for a race he kept rubbing his neck. I thought to myself, "I did that to him." I can't have done him much harm – I think he won a bronze medal.

'So whatever it says in the record books is wrong – my first fight in the 1984 Olympics was against Ben Johnson.'

His first official opponent managed to do more damage than the sprinter. Lennox showed his inexperience in his opening bout when he was caught flat-footed at the bell. Pakistan's Mohammad Yousuf almost ran from his stool and waded in, forcing Lennox to take a standing eight count after he had fielded a solid right.

But after that flurry the outcome was never in doubt. Lennox settled down to box, and scored with solid combinations. In the third round Lennox landed a lightning right hand which felled Yousuf, and the fight was over with 1 minute 43 seconds left.

'I deserved the standing count because I was caught off guard by the way Yousuf came charging at me at the bell. He fazed me, but he didn't daze me,' said Lennox then. 'I was only happy with the way I boxed in the third round. I'll get better and better from this point on. I came ready to fight, but the five-day wait kind of took the edge off my preparations. Now that I've had this first fight I'm ready again.'

In the next round Lennox was drawn against the favourite. The night before, he studied tapes of Biggs on a video in the Olympic village. 'From what I've seen, I'm convinced I can beat him,' he told pressmen.

But the big occasion got to him, and he froze. Arnie Boehm recalls, 'For someone so inexperienced, Lennox had done very well against the Pakistani guy. He was huge – a monster – but, after that initial set-back and the eight count, Lennox kept his cool and was way ahead when he finished him off.

'But when it came to the big one his lack of international exposure showed. He didn't sleep the previous night. Not that he was afraid, but the aura and anticipation of the big event got to him.

'To show how it affected him, when I was warming him up in the dressing-room he was so tensed-up he could hardly coordinate his punches. We would do different combinations and he would hit my hands. Left hook, left hook, right hand, left hook, and so on. I called, "Right hand, left hook," and he reversed it. He threw a left hook first and caught me right on the chin. He apologized and was upset. I said, "You're pretty nervous, aren't you?" He wouldn't say so, but I knew.'

In the fight, Lennox never really got into his rhythm. He started tentatively, showing all his nerves. Although he got better the longer the fight went on, at the end he clearly hadn't done enough and the judges gave it unanimously to Biggs. At least Lennox had the hollow consolation of being beaten by the eventual winner – Biggs took the gold from Damiani in the final.

'Biggs wasn't better than me – it was just that he had more experience. Every time I set myself to hit him he had moved away,' says Lennox. 'He was very elusive. But the more the fight went on, the more I was getting to him. I had him figured out by the end of the fight, but by then it was too late as far as my medal hopes went.'

'Lennox showed how much of an apprentice he still was,' says Boehm. 'If it had been a club fight in a small gym Lennox would have beaten him easily. But because it was a big occasion, watched by all the world, his nerves got to him. Lennox had far more skill, and a bigger heart than Biggs – he just couldn't match him in experience. It was Lennox's seventh senior international bout, whereas Biggs had been in an international ring a dozen times. If they'd fought again the next day Lennox would have won. He always had the beating of him – and he proved that when they met as professionals.

'In a way I'm glad he didn't win that fight. If he'd got to the final and won a gold medal the pressure on him to turn professional would have been too strong. I thought he wasn't yet old enough to turn pro. He had time on his side, and I wanted him to progress bit by bit and get more experience. The professional game is very tough, and if you get there when you're not quite ready they can chew you up and spit you out. The last person I wanted that to happen to was Lennox.'

5

Cheer for Me

The start of the love-affair between Lennox Lewis and his girlfriend of ten year's standing, Marcia Miller, could have come line by line straight from a pop song about teenage romance. She was sweet little sixteen. He was the leader of the pack. Then, Zap! – let's get it on!

They first met in 1983. She was a raven-haired, black-eyed cheerleader for the Eastwood Collegiate basketball squad in Kitchener. He was the 6 feet 3 inch, seventeen-year-old star player with their arch-rivals Cameron Heights. One day their eyes met across a crowded basketball court and – Slam dunk! – there was instant electricity between them. Or at least a bright spark.

His version: 'It was funny because she was supposed to be a cheerleader for Eastwood, but every time I scored for Cameron when we played Eastwood she cheered for me. She was hounded by everyone in Kitchener. It's a small place, and all the boys were saying they wanted to go out with her. She was pretty, and we all liked her because she had a nice personality too. At one time everybody was after her, so I never was.

'She used to go to Temple Baptist Church. They had a competition there once among the kids to see who could get the most people to come to church. A whole lot of people went with her – a bus-load of kids. Boys and girls, but mostly boys. She phoned me to ask me to go to church with her, but I never went.

49

'Then there was a drop in the number of times I saw her. She was going out with Toronto boys, because they were more sophisticated – guys with cars from out of town. That's what I thought she was like.

'One day we were playing a basketball game at her school. She was walking down the hall and I put my arm round her and I said, "I think you're really nice. Make sure you cheer for me." And after that I started to pester her. I went through her brother, Milton. It's the Jamaican way. I told him, "I like your sister." I told all her friends that she was very nice. I knew it would get back to her.

'Then one day there was a demonstration of break-dancing at Fairview Mall. I did the chicken-and-popping part. Then I was doing a bit of crowd control. I saw her and walked her home. I said, "Are you going to give me a kiss goodbye?" She said, "No." I said to her brother, "I walk her all the way home and she can't even give me a kiss on the cheek." He told her, "Just give him a kiss," and that was the beginning of the whole thing.'

Her version: 'When he put his arm around me in the gym he told me that he thought I was the best-looking girl in the school. But I didn't believe it, and I just ignored him. Then after that he started telling my brother and all my best friends that they should encourage me to talk to him. He tried to get to everybody that was close to me. I thought to myself, "I'll talk to him as a friend, but that's all." Then a couple of months later we started going out.

On my seventeenth birthday, on 25 June, he took a whole load of us out to Bingeman Park in his coach Arnie's van. Bingeman Park's got a water park, go-karts, a golf course, roller-skating and a whole lot of amusements. We all went down the water slide, but he waited for us at the bottom because he thought he was too big to fit on the slide.

'My parents were very strict, and he always had to have me home by a certain time. At first I wasn't attracted to him. I didn't even like him. He was so big – like a giant. I was intimidated by that. When they were doing the drive at my church for us all to invite people to join us in the congregation, I didn't even invite him, and he wasn't too thrilled about that.

'The first time he came to our house he brought candy for my little sisters. He tried to put on a really good show, and he was very polite to my mother, Pearl. That was always important, to impress my mother. All we did the first time he came to my house was sit in the kitchen and draw pictures and talk. I suppose if we have an anniversary it's 15 March. We always celebrate that every year, because that's the date on which we started to talk to each other.'

His version: 'Our first big date was her seventeenth birthday. I got all dressed up and was looking very smart. I'd borrowed Arnie's van, and we'd planned to go to Bingeman Park. I thought we were going on our own, as a date, but when I got to her house there were about sixteen people there – all her friends and relatives. So I had to take a whole van-load of people, plus her, on the date. It was a big shock that first date. She was very nice. I watched her go down the water slide. In fact I watched a whole van-load of people go down a water slide. It was funny. We still laugh about it.

'Her mother was always very protective of her – at one stage guys couldn't even get past the front door. But I think the family liked boxing and the fact that I was doing something constructive with my life. Her mum liked me for that.

'So our friendship just grew from there. We'd phone each other and see each other a lot. Then when I was in Toronto training for the Olympics in '88, and she was in college there, we saw each other a great deal. We never officially lived together, but I always had the key to her apartment.'

Their friendship survived – even thrived – after his decision to base his professional career in Britain. They would see each other in Canada whenever possible for romantic reunions. They regularly holidayed together in Jamaica, and spent weekends in New York. Marcia was nearly always there as a guest at his important fights. In 1992, while on holiday in Jamaica, Lennox gave her a ring. 'I looked on it that we were engaged to be engaged,' he says. She accepted the ring – a pear-shaped diamond. Then in January 1993 their romance faltered. They are still the best of friends. She has kept his ring, but doesn't actually wear it. For the moment he rules out marriage, but says that he still cares for her very much.

In many ways they are like an old married couple. They have pet names for each other. They call each other Booga, without being able to define what it means. She also calls him Precious, or Junior – his name from school. Before each fight she generally sends him eleven red roses, with an odd white or yellow one. Once for his birthday she decorated a hotel room with a 'Happy Birthday' banner and told him there were some friends there waiting for him. When he arrived there was a cake in the bathtub and she was there alone. 'I surprised him by myself.' she says. Like a long-suffering wife she can also list his annoying habits: flicking from channel to channel with the TV remote control; flooding the bathroom every time he takes a shower, waking up everybody in the house as soon as he opens his eyes. (She can provide a full list on application.)

The versions of the current state of their relationship, and the reasons for their differences, are, like the accounts of their first meetings, still slightly out of kilter.

Marcia is now twenty-seven. She is beautiful, with a coffee-cream complexion. She has been a model, and now teaches modelling. She has a degree in public relations, and has studied broadcast journalism in Hamilton, Ontario. She says, 'In May 1992 I had just graduated from my broadcast-journalism course and we went on holiday together to Jamaica. [It was after Lennox had won the Common-wealth championship from Derek Williams.]

'We were staying at a house when Lennox gave me the ring. We had just had dinner and we were in the jacuzzi. I'm very daring and outgoing, and I was in the pool. He said, "I'm going to dim the lights." I said, "OK, well hurry up," because I was scared as it was an outside pool. It was late at night, and I'm thinking, "What's taking this man so long to come back?" Then there was this little black box floating around in the water. I thought it was a speaker or something, because he's into music and always has gadgets for his speaker system.

The floating box contained the ring with a pear-shaped diamond, and Marcia accepted it. 'I think I know him just about better than anybody, because I have been with him for ten years. We are very close, and we love each other very much. I have seen him at his weakest and his strongest points.

'I remember when he used to spar with Razor Ruddock in Toronto. One day when they had sparred he wasn't pleased with his performance. He came back to my house and he was so angry. He said, "Marcia, it's never going to happen again. Whenever I get a chance to fight this man I'm going to beat him badly." That was five years before he met Razor as a professional and beat him in two rounds, but I always knew he would do it.

'He's always been convinced that one day he would be a success. If he says he's going to do something he generally achieves it. I think he's a great inspiration in that way to me. A long time ago – long before he won his Olympic gold medal we'd be driving along the highway in Toronto and he'd say, "You know what, Marcia? One day I'm going to be the heavyweight champion of the world and I'm going to make a lot of money.' And he so believed he would do it that I believed it too.

'Whenever I watch him fight there are so many different emotions going through my head. There's excitement. There's fear. Tension. Anxiety. So many different feelings. I know it can be dangerous, and I'd hate for anything to happen to him. But because he's so good he's never been really hurt, so I haven't had to deal with a very bad experience.

'Watching him is scary and electrifying at the same time. My stomach's churning, and I'm yelling. Then at the end of it all I'm relieved, elated and exhausted. I don't think Lennox really addresses the dangerous side of the sport. He always thinks positively. He says, "Don't worry about it." I do worry. But I always tell him if he came home with no teeth and a cut eye I'd still love him.'

They are still very friendly, but decided to end their relationship at the start of 1993. Lennox explains, 'We've broken up officially, but never mentally. We still meet. I suppose it's geography that got between us more than anything else. She's there and I'm moving all over the world and we don't have much chance to meet each other.

'The problem was that while I was in training camp I heard stories that she was going out and meeting other guys at social events. She has a best friend called Lorna Allinan whom I don't like. I call Lorna CNN, because she spends most of her time broadcasting our news all over the place. The last thing I wanted to hear when I was in training was that Marcia was out with Lorna partying.'

What came between the engagement and the break-up was the world title, and Marcia thinks that that changed things between them. 'So much has changed so quickly for us,' she says. 'We went from being an everyday steady relationship to suddenly him being world champion. We had to make certain adjustments about what to expect from each other, and they were difficult. Suddenly our expectations seemed to be different, and I guess we weren't making each other happy. We certainly weren't as happy as we were before.

'When he came to Canada I expected him to spend time with me. But he had so many things to do and so many people to see that sometimes I just felt left out of his life. He wants a lot of respect, and says I don't have a lot of respect for him. I do, but I hardly get a chance to show it – everything was so temperamental, everything was so up in the air. It was difficult.

'We still love each other very much. We've grown apart in some ways, but there's still a lot of love there. I love him to the bone. I probably would marry him, as we've always talked about it. I've saved myself from getting pregnant until we were married, as opposed to having a child out of wedlock.

'Sometimes I get jealous. But he knows that I'm with him for the right reasons. He knows that I'll say to him, "Look, I understand the position you're in. I understand there's going to be a lot of women around." But I just trust him to know how far to take things.

'How his mum views me is a very good question. It's not that his mum doesn't like me – his mum is protective of anybody around Lennox Lewis. It's like she kind of 'scopes everybody. Lennox is like her baby, and she's still cautious of any- and everybody. Really I sometimes think that I don't get enough credit, as I'm not there to hurt him in any way. The relationship with her could be better, put it that way.

'Our best times are when it's still just me and him together. We sit down, we're very affectionate with each other. We just cuddle and talk about everything that's going on in our lives.

'I almost feel like I've been married to him. It's been total commitment and, looking back on the ten years, I feel I could conquer anything now after being with him. Looking back on the ten years, I feel very durable.'

As for Lennox, he says, 'With her and me – but especially her – it's not like we're really over. There's still that chemistry there. But when people say, "Do you love her?" – what is love? People's interpretations of love are so different. Wanting. Needing. Can't do without. I can do without – yes. But I care for her very deeply – like a sister now. If somebody insulted her or slapped her I'd get outraged like any brother. So when I understand what love is, then I'll answer. But I do still want to spend time with Marcia. We do have that kind of zest between us.'

The downfall of great heavyweights has always been drugs, booze, crooked managers, a fight too many, serious injury and conniving, avaricious women. Lennox says his aim is to become one of the few champions in fight history to steer clear of all six hazards.

Marcia Miller met him and grew to love him when he was penniless. Now he is a champion and a millionaire, and there is no guarantee that for any new woman coming into his life the attraction won't be the money, rather than the man. Robin Givens was married briefly to Mike Tyson. When they divorced she was awarded their $1.5 million home in the Hollywood Hills and several million dollars' worth of assets.

'I do see it as a danger. It's very difficult,' says Lennox. 'I don't want to get caught up in a Robin Givens situation. I always look at women as being dangerous – more dangerous than boxing. Both can affect you mentally, but women can be more dangerous – especially if you allow them to get to you.

'I'm always wary of women. You can never really know what people's motives are, but I believe my vibes will tell me when I meet the right girl. My mum is always good when it comes to that. In a sense I trust my mum's opinion, because you may have many girls but you only have one mother. My mother has weeded out certain girls in my life, given me her motherly advice. The girlfriend always gets introduced to mum. Always. Definitely.'

Lennox wants to start a family very soon. He's already chosen a boy's name, his own special creation: Ifnox. 'Ifnox – isn't that horrible?' squeals Marcia. 'He swears blind he's going to name our son Ifnox,'

Will Lennox and Marcia settle their differences? Will Marcia and mum make up? Will the former cheerleader ever get her boxer down the aisle? There are the markings of a soap opera here, and a lucrative gambling opportunity for Ladbroke's. The outcome of the Lennox love stakes would make an interesting bet.

6

Trying to Run
a Racing-car on Coal

For a perfectionist like Lennox, elimination from the 1984 Olympics was failure. Even so, he returned home to a tempting $500,000 dollar offer from an American manager to turn professional – as Mike Tyson had just done.

The lure came from Mike Jones, co-manager of Gerry Cooney and manager of the WBC super-lightweight champion Billy Costello. He was one of the most trustworthy and respected managers in boxing, and when he died tragically early, in 1990, Muhammad Ali's biographer Thomas Hauser wrote of him, 'In a business where most people have only allies, he had friends. His word was good: he never walked out on a deal.'

The Brooklyn-born Jones thought he could groom the teenage Lennox into a champion. In spite of his friendliness and patent honesty, and the offer of what was an astronomical signing fee for a young man just turning nineteen, he failed to take Lewis to America. Lennox had a conference with Arnie and his mum and decided it was more important to graduate from high school.

'For someone so young who didn't have an Olympic medal it was a fabulous offer,' says Lennox. 'But we felt that after getting some Olympic experience I should do better next time round. I really wanted to remain amateur until 1988, because I thought I would be in with a very good chance for a medal.

'None of the people I spoke to thought I was ready to turn pro yet. I hadn't finished school, and that was more important. He tried to tempt me. He said I could break a hand and miss the next Olympics, there could be a boycott – anything could happen. He was putting all those thoughts in my head. Plus the offer of half a million, Canadian.

'It was really my choice, but I took advice from Arnie. He was very worried about me signing contracts. He was very protective of me, and I listened to him because I respected his judgement. So we said no to the half million.'

When he left school, apart from a few casual jobs, Lennox spent most of his time boxing and training. There were times in the next four years when that signing-on fee would have been handy. In the run-up to Seoul he was fighting for financial survival, and fending off carping criticism about his motivation.

Money worries not only threatened his chances of winning a medal, they also got him embroiled in a bitter management wrangle which soured negotiations when he eventually decided to turn professional in 1988.

Several events conspired to give him major problems. In the summer of 1985 lack of financial support from the city of Kitchener forced Arnie Boehm to close the Waterloo Regional Police Boxing Association. The WRPBA had been one of the most successful breeding grounds of Canadian boxing talent since the 1950s, but when cash flow slowed to a trickle, and community politicians declined to help, Boehm decided he'd had enough and took a coaching job with Boxing Canada in Toronto.

Boehm's preoccupation with boxing had cost him his job with the electricity company, forcing him to work as a self-employed line man. His employers had issued an ultimatum at the time of the World Junior Championships in November 1983. Arnie recalls, 'The utility would not let me take time off at my own expense. They said, "If you go, you're suspended," and, me being the obstinate person I am, I went and got suspended.'

Depressed at the loss of his job and his boxing club, Arnie turned to drink. 'When I was discouraged, sometimes I'd hide in the bottle,' he says, 'I've still got the alcoholic problem, except that now I don't drink. At the time, I hit the bottle pretty hard,. But I could never fool Lennox. The moment he talked to me on the telephone – even if I only said, "Hello" – he would know I was drinking. Yet he accepted my alcoholism as a sickness. He detested the disease itself, but he never put me down for it.

'I gave him a hard time,' says Lennox. 'I'd say, "Arnie, what are you doing to yourself?" I wouldn't have to say much, but he seemed to listen if I told him to stop. He would gradually stop if the boxing kids gave him an incentive to stop and concentrate on us.'

The end of the boxing club meant that several outstanding Kitchener boxers – Lewis, Greg Johnson and Wayne Thompson – had nowhere to train locally.

Boehm drove the trio back and forth the 60 miles to Toronto, but, having done their sparring, the boxers then had to wait until Arnie had finished his long coaching sessions before they could cadge a ride home.

Lennox had to sit around for hours waiting for his lift. He was getting to bed late and surviving on take-aways picked up on the late-night drive home. It was no way to prepare for one of the most demanding events in the Olympic calendar. Eventually Lennox tired of commuting to training and moved into a mate's flat in Toronto.

Most high-performance Olympic athletes cannot achieve the peak of fitness and skill they require for their sport while holding down a regular job. The Corinthian ideal of the plucky amateur that so enthused Baron Pierre de Coubertin is as long gone as Tom Brown's schooldays. Current Olympians are professionals in all but name, surviving on sponsorship, government grants and some good old-fashioned hat-passing. (For years Arnie's wife Verna had kept his boxing club in the black with weekly bingo sessions.)

What made things even worse for Lennox was that he had failed to get A-card status at the World Amateur Championships in Reno, Nevada, in May 1986. Sports Canada, which awards grants to promising champions, calculated what it paid out solely on performance in the Olympics and the World Championships.

By losing a hotly disputed 3–2 split decision to Bulgaria's Peter Stoinomov, Lewis was granted C-card status, which meant that he received only $450 a month in expense money from Sports Canada. If he'd got past the opening rounds he would have been awarded $100 dollars more as a B-card man. If he'd finished among the top four he would have been entitled to $650 a month as an A-card athlete.

What made it even more galling was that he lost the fight to Reno, which many thought he had won, only on the casting vote of an Eastern-bloc judge. Then, a couple of months later in July 1986, he picked up the gold at the Commonwealth Games in Edinburgh by knocking out the 6 feet 9 inch James Oyebola of England in the second round, and going on to beat Welshman Aneurin Evans in the final. But those thumping victories, which underlined his Olympic credentials, did not count in Sports Canada's ratings.

'The games in Edinburgh was a good tournament for me,' says Lennox. 'I heard through the grapevine that some of the coaches had bet against me in the Oyebola fight. He was huge, and everyone was saying, "Oh no, you won't go past him." He looked very intimidating. I took a look at him in the dining-room, and he had a huge physique. He was built like a house. But when I come up against a tough proposition it generally brings the best out of me. I rise to the occasion.

'The fight was strange, because I was throwing out jabs and he was throwing out jabs at the same time. But he was jolting my head back because his arms were so much longer than mine. So I said to myself, "Forget this. Go inside." And I threw all boxing out of the window and just got after him, Rambo style. And I knocked him out.'

After Edinburgh, Lennox went down to London to see his brother, Dennis. 'He didn't know I was coming – I just turned up on his front door,' he says. 'We got on very well. The feeling was like we'd never been separated. He was doing some DJ work at the time and took me around a lot of clubs. He was introducing me as his brother. People were saying, "I didn't know you had a brother, but, now you come to say it, you do look alike." We got to know each other a lot more as brothers, and we had a good time.'

He also visited his father, Carlton Brooks. Lennox says, 'We got on fine, there was no animosity. But apart from the fact that he was my father we didn't have much in common. He had two daughters, and I think he would have liked me to get to know his family. But, after so many years being brought up by my mother on her own, I didn't see much point in it.' (Later, after Lennox's 1988 Olympic success, his father wrote congratulating him. They remained civil, but at arm's length.)

Back home, Lennox tried to keep his dream of an Olympic gold alive in spite of the set-backs. But a government cheque of $450 a month barely covered basic expenses such as food and rent. He couldn't afford a car of his own. He was also having difficulty in finding sparring partners who would stretch his growing talent. Lennox says, 'At one stage I felt a bit like an ice-hockey player trying to play without any ice.'

The training programme a heavyweight boxer needs doesn't come cheap. You're not supposed to hone yourself to a peak of physical fitness in this rough-hewn trade on junk food, but special vitamins, diet supplements – even a good steak – were beyond his budget. At times it felt like he was trying to run a grand-prix racing-car on coal.

At this low point, when his morale was under attack, he admits he had been tempted by several offers to turn professional. 'I tried to stay positive, but I saw guys like Ruddock and Biggs making the big bucks as pros and it got me down at times. But I was still trying to concentrate on the Olympics. I was young, and I realized time was on my side. Besides, how many boxers get the opportunity to compete in two Olympics?'

He was also annoyed that the atmosphere surrounding Canada's brightest 1988 medal prospects was lukewarm compared to the national excitement that had gripped the country in 1984. He doubted whether the average Canadian had even heard of him or of middleweight Egerton Marcus. Four years earlier huge media attention had focused on white fighters Shawn O'Sullivan and Willie de Wit. Before their silver-medal performances at Los Angeles, de Wit and O'Sullivan were household names.

Black fighters are not as marketable as white fighters in a world where every promoter is searching for a Great White Hope. But there seemed more to it than plain economics. Ask Lennox if he thinks racism was responsible for the lack of attention before Seoul and there is a long pause. 'Yes,' he says, and then changes the subject.

Between the games of 1984 and 1988 there was no one to match Lennox's power in Canada, but his international results were erratic, showing that he still had some learning to do. He had impressive victories at the Commonwealth Games in 1986 and at the Felix Stamm Tournament in Warsaw in November 1987, but there were key defeats against Ulli Kaden in the World Cup in Belgrade in October 1987 and against Alexander Morischnichenco in the Intercup in Karlsruhe five months before Seoul.

'He was never badly beaten. No one ever knocked him over,' says Arnie Boehm, 'You've got to remember that he was still a young man learning his trade. In Canada there wasn't really anyone who could pose him any difficult questions in the ring. The learning-curve went up when he boxed guys from abroad – and he was a quick learner. Every time he's had a rematch with someone who's beaten him, Lennox has got his revenge.

'And then again,' he laughs, 'sometimes when he lost it seemed like daylight robbery.'

One example of that was the Pan-American Games at Indianapolis in August 1987, when he lost on a 4–1 decision to the Cuban Jorge Gonzales. The American judge made Lennox a clear winner, but he was outvoted 4–1 by four Latin American judges. Lennox joked afterwards, 'The decision really surprised me, but I think it surprised Jorge even more.' But Lennox had the last laugh – later the same month he decisively beat Gonzales in the North American Championships.

More worrying as Seoul approached were the opinions – increasingly voiced among some critics – that, for all his natural ability, Lennox had intangible shortcomings. They claimed he was dilatory, too laid-back; that he lacked the big-fight temperament.

Even Mike Jones, the manager who had tried to sign him, was critical. 'He's in shape all the time, and he's a tremendous athlete. The only drawback I've seen in his attitude,' he said.

'One night he looks like a million dollars,' said Dennis Bradley of Boxing Ontario, 'the rest of the time he looks like a bum. Lennox is his own worst enemy. He's so lackadaisical.' Even the Canadian national team coach, Taylor Gordon, while admitting Lennox's ability, questioned his heart.

The accusations bring a stinging rebuff from his coach at Seoul, Adrian Teodorescu. 'I never had a problem with Lennox. His attitude with me in the gym was always 100 per cent positive. When people were accusing him of being lazy, I told them, "First of all you don't know what you're talking about. And, second, you don't know a thing about Lennox."

'Lennox isn't a flyweight who can jump around like a grasshopper. He's a wonderful athlete, he's quick and nimble, but the guy's a heavyweight – you can't expect him to buzz like a flyweight.

'All I could tell them is that he always worked hard for me. The first training camp I took him to was Lake Placid, and he worked so hard he got this huge blister on his foot. Other people would have complained, but he kept on working right through the pain barrier. That's when I realized he had the makings of a champion.'

Other people realized that Lennox was a potential world-beater and, for reasons of community spirit – larded with a fair streak of self-interest – rallied round.

In November 1986 a consortium of Kitchener businessmen started a campaign to raise funds to support Lennox's training. Bob Neufeld, the owner of the local Emerald Limousine Service and a partner in a pensions and insurance group, launched a Lennox Lewis '88 Gold Fund. It had a target of $164,000 to pay for items like vitamins, sparring, medical expenses and coaching costs that Lennox would have to find on the two-year run-up to Seoul.

Neufeld had been a fascinated spectator when Lewis and several other boxers went to the University of Waterloo to have their punching power electronically monitored. 'I remember all the little guys went up first to the machine they had rigged up there,' he said. 'They always like to start with the small guys and build up to the bigger guys in boxing.

'They all went through fine, and then it was Lennox's turn. When he finally got up there he hit the machine so hard that he busted it and sent it right across the room.

'No one in the world can match his punching power, and I really mean that. Not even Mike Tyson.'

Launching his appeal, Neufeld asked the home-town folks to dig deep into their pockets. 'We have one of the best in the world right here in our home town,' he said, 'and I decided it was time someone had to jump in and help him. I didn't realize how badly off he was until I met with him a few days ago.

'He doesn't eat right and he doesn't have the proper equipment. He's a totally dedicated kid, and I want to do what I can to help. It's a big job, though. I've already made some corporate contacts, and if we tell the story right I think we can get some action.'

But the story wasn't told right. The fund fell far short of its $164,000 target figure and the project was abandoned. A problem was that most of the $71,000 raised was in goods and services – only $6,000 was in cash. 'We're broke, and Lennox has been getting by on hand-outs,' Neufeld said at the time.

Less than a year later, in July 1987, Neufeld resurfaced with another money-making scheme for his favourite boxer. The plan to sell a hundred $5,000 (Canadian) shares in the Lennox Jr Lewis Corporation never really got off the ground. The idea was that, if Lennox made $2 million in his first year as a professional after Seoul, the shareholders would get their $5,000 back and be up by a further $1,000 by the autumn of 1989. But complications arose with the Ontario Securities Commission, and no money exchanged hands. Names of some of the other people involved in the scheme would crop up in another grandiose project to turn Lennox into a gilt-edged professional asset after the Seoul games, though.

Teodorescu, a Romanian émigré ('I was never a member of the Communist Party, even if they call me a Communist dictator in the gym') was a coach to the Canadian boxing team at the Seoul and Barcelona Olympics. He is a man with a warm Transylvanian smile and, if not the last word, certainly the next to last word in Central European charm. He got close to Lennox, seeing himself as a teacher, friend and Svengali figure.

In March 1988 he set up a scheme in which a group of businessmen – of whom the main one was David Hurst, the boss of a Toronto metal-finishing business and uncle of a promising Canadian boxer, Nick Ruppa – covered the living and training expenses of Lennox and Egerton Marcus, another bright Olympic-medal prospect. The backers also provided down payments to buy each boxer a car – Lewis a Thunderbird, Marcus a Firebird.

It was all done in a way that would not endanger the boxers' amateur status and Olympic eligibility. The rules of the Association Internationale de Boxe Amateur – the world body that oversees amateur boxing – forbid fighters from signing professional contracts or receiving money from professional boxing organizations while they are amateurs, although they are not barred from borrowing funds to cover their expenses. (Lennox's personal expenses from Hurst were a relatively modest $200 a week.)

The boxers were lent the money at an annual interest rate of 15 per cent. But there was also a penalty clause included in the deal. If the loan was not repaid in full by 31 May 1988 – only two months after signing the agreement and four months before the Olympics, at a time when both men were still amateurs and earning no money – each could owe $100,000 (Canadian). This was clearly an incentive to induce them to sign professionally after Korea, with the understanding that all the debts would be forgotten just as long as Egerton and Lennox signed to the group.

At the time it seemed a friendly enough arrangement. The agreement set out the basis for a management company that would handle the fighters' pro careers. It was called Mallet Sports Inc. – an acronym from the three main players' initials: Marcus, Adrian, Lennox, Lewis, Egerton, Teodorescu.

Neither boxer was aware of the full implications of the papers they had put their names to; both had signed without a lawyer's advice. All that mattered to them was that now they could put their full energy into training for the Olympics unburdened by day-to-day money worries.

Lennox and Egerton had made the kind of elementary mistake that ambitious but unsophisticated boxers are always making: they had signed a paper without fully understanding it.

For now, Lewis and Marcus were preoccupied with the Olympics. The essential inequity of their business arrangement would only be brought home to them later. As the boxers trained, the one-sided deal was a time bomb primed to go off. It would explode when they returned from the Olympics with their medals and refused to sign with Mallet.

7

See You in the Pros

Seoul '88 will always be remembered as the Olympics when Ben Johnson went from hero to zero in 9.79 seconds and Lennox Lewis took not much longer to power his way in the other direction, to glory.

In the most dramatic run in the history of the human race, Ben Johnson exploded from the blocks, powered past a field that included his hated rival Carl Lewis, and ran across the finishing-line with one hand held high. Then came the failed drugs test and disgrace. He was stripped of his gold medal and shipped home like a convict, pursued by the world's media.

Canada was gripped by a spasm of public shame. The human cheetah was a cheater.

A week later a walloping right-arm from Lennox Lewis restored a semblance of national pride. The punch snapped back the head of Riddick Bowe, and the East German referee, Gustav Baumgardt, stepped between the two fighters. He gave the dazed American a standing count of eight, and, as it was the second compulsory count of the round, it was all over. Bowe raised his arms in an attempt to show he wasn't hurt, but the referee waved him to his corner and defeat.

With that dynamic right hand Lennox had ended fifty-six years of Canadian boxing frustration. The country had taken its first boxing gold medal since Horace 'Lefty' Gwynne won the bantamweight title at the 1932 Olympics.

Bowe's first mistake had happened twenty-four hours before he stepped into the ring. He gave a boastfully overconfident interview to NBC the night before the fight. Lennox watched the interview on a television in the Olympic village as he was relaxing in his quarters. What he heard hardened his already steely resolve.

'Bowe was speaking as though it was a mere formality for him to pick up the gold medal. He said he was going to go after me and then turn professional and seek out the [then] undefeated Mike Tyson.

'I was thinking, "Him go after me? I'm stronger than him. I'm a better boxer than him." He was talking about taking me to school, but I knew he'd have to put up in the ring against me.

'What upset me was that the Americans were hyping him up, saying, "All he's got to do is beat the Canadian." It was like no other country mattered in the Games but America.'

Lennox's coach and cornerman Adrian Teodorescu – then a veteran of six Olympics – knew that his man was in perfect physical and psychological shape. 'We knew that Bowe would not be an easy fight, but I was 100 per cent confident that Lennox was able to take him, because his previous performances had been awesome in their power.'

Before he reached Seoul there had been an injury scare. In June, in his final match before the Olympics, he broke his right thumb in the Canada Cup. He knocked out Elton Wright of the USA in the first round of the final, but one of his big puches hit the American hard on the headgear and broke the tip of Lewis's thumb.

'It was a worry for a while, but it didn't take long to heal,' he says. 'Breaking it was actually a blessing in disguise. It made me use my left jab more than I ever did before. I use my left hand most of the time. The right hand is just for finishing off.'

In Korea, the right hand proved that it could finish off in very short order: Lennox won his gold in under three rounds.

His first bout saw him comprehensively outclass Crispine Odera of Kenya, felling him to the canvas in round one, almost before ringsiders had settled in their seats. Then in the quarter-finals he demolished Germany's world champion Ullie Kaden in 34 seconds of the first round. He came roaring out of his corner eager to get his revenge on the man who had beaten him in the World Cup in Belgrade the previous autumn. The East German had been highly touted for the gold medal, yet he wilted under Lennox's all-out barrage. Lewis worked up to the knockout with a display of punching power. He overwhelmed the German with solid lefts and rights, finally putting him away with a long left.

'I wanted to win badly – really badly,' says Lennox. 'I was talking to Adrian before the fight, and he said, 'Show no respect. Get out there and kill.' When he beat me in the World Cup I thought it was one of those political decisions you get in the amateurs. I was sure I had beaten him.

'For this one I really psyched myself up, saying, "He's going to have to knock me out to win this." I came straight out of my corner and just went Rambo again.'

After the fight, Lennox phoned Arnie Boehm in Kitchener with the good news. 'When they met in the World Cup, Lennox had Kaden on the floor twice and they still gave the decision to the German,' says Arnie. 'Lennox never complains when a result goes against him, but afterwards he said to me, "Arnie, I know I won that fight." But when he got the second chance in Seoul he made no mistake.

'He called me and he was so happy – just ecstatic. He said, "Arnie, that right hand was for you." I said to him, "Lennox. I have a question. Thirty-four seconds. What took you so long?" '

'Our strategy was to knock him out,' says Teodorescu – 'That way there is no argument about who is the winner. We didn't want to give the judges a chance to rob us if it went to a decision.'

Teodorescu came to distrust the judges' ability to spot a winner. When the boxing tournament finished in Korea there was so much controversy about bad decisions that it seemed to some observers that amateur boxing would be excluded from future Olympics. International Olympic Committee president Juan Antonio Samarach had stated publicly that he would like to see the sport dropped, and the events in Korea can only have strengthened his resolve.

First there was a riot in the ring when irate Korean officials attacked a New Zealand referee who had dared to penalize one of their boxers, who was subsequently declared a loser on points. Then the boxer concerned refused to accept the decision, staging a sit-down strike in the ring for over an hour even when the lights of the arena were turned off.

The simultaneous use of two rings brought chaos, with boxers confused by a cacophony of bells and unable to tell when their rounds were starting or stopping. But the nadir was some of the worst verdicts in the history of the sport. The judges were about as good as the Venus de Milo directing traffic.

The tournament ended in bitter controversy when Korean light-middleweight Park Si-hun was awarded a 3–2 decision over the USA's Roy Jones. The Soviet and Hungarian judges made Jones a 60–56 winner, but the three others – from Uruguay, Uganda and Morocco – surprisingly chose the local man. To make it worse, after his 'defeat' Jones was awarded the Val Barker Trophy for the outstanding boxer of the tournament – a prize that invariably goes to the winner of the gold medal.

Lennox boxed his final straight after the diabolical Jones decision and was worried in case it turned the judges against him. 'I was in the gloving-up room ready to come out when Jones was robbed of that fight,' he says, 'I was next on, and thought to myself, "There's bound to be sympathy for the next American boxer. They'll want to make it up to the Americans for Jones being robbed." I thought the only way to make sure I won was to knock Bowe out.'

Most boxers at the Olympics went in fear of shambolic judges. It was even reported that a Korean had given presents to some of the judges. One verdict left a Yugoslav cornerman laughing ironically; another had the Italian Vincenzo Nardiello beating the canvas with rage. (He had been 'outpointed' by Park Si-hun too.) If they'd had these Olympic judges in the Book of David, Goliath would have won on a split decision.

In the quarter-finals, Janusz Zarenkiewicz of Poland had outpointed Schnieders of West Germany and was due to meet Lennox in the semifinal. But he pulled out of the fight at the last minute, informing officials that he had damaged his hand.

'Zarenkiewicz knew Lennox of old, and there is no way he would have been eager to fight him,' says Teodorescu. 'We'd been at a training camp in Poland a year earlier, and Lennox broke him to pieces in sparring. The day before the tournament in Warsaw the guy just left the training camp and disappeared. He didn't want to participate, because he knew that in a fight with Lennox he had no chance of winning.

'From our point of view that was ideal, because it gave Lennox an extra recovery period before the final. But it wouldn't have mattered – Lennox would have taken him out as impressively as he dealt with Kaden, he was in such great physical shape.'

There were only eighteen big men in the super-heavyweight class, and that meant long gaps between fights and lots of boredom and inactivity. An Olympic village is a strange place, full of self-absorbed athletes, those who have yet to compete being in a Zen-like trance as they contemplate their event, and those who have already won or lost noisily letting off steam.

'The big problem is mental stress. Boredom is the big enemy of boxers,' Lennox says. 'Waiting around for days on end gives you too much time to think about things. You're bored and tensed up at the same time. What you want is the fights to come as quickly as possible, so that you can dispose of one man and turn your attentions to the next. In the big amateur tournaments, unless you're nursing an injury, the quicker the fights come the better it is for the boxer.

The night Ben Johnson won his scorching 100 metres, and before news of the drugs scandal broke, Lewis was so excited by it he wished he'd been scheduled to fight right away.

'It seemed like such a fantastic victory. The whole Canadian camp was buzzing. I was really lifted by it. Nobody would have lasted with me that night. Then, when we found out about the steroids, it was such a disappointment. I remember I was sleeping when one of the other boxers came into my room and told me. I didn't think he'd do something like that. I was disappointed in him, but sad for him at the same time.

'One thing I didn't like was the way Canadians turned on him. When he won the gold they were proud to call him a Canadian. When the drugs thing came out and he was disgraced they went back to calling him a Jamaican. Taking an illegal substance was wrong. The tragedy was he was a great athlete and didn't need to do that. It just left a bad taste with me the way people turned on him. He should have received much more support.

'After his disgrace, the atmosphere in the Canadian quarters was paranoid. In the area in the village where we were staying, athletes were hiding. People who usually wore their Canadian jerseys or track suits weren't wearing them. They didn't want to be beseiged by reporters asking how the team felt. There was a board of honour downstairs where they listed all the people who had won medals for Canada. After the Johnson thing, even that was taken down.

The final against Bowe went almost as the coach and boxer had planned it. 'We had seen all the tapes of Bowe fighting before we got to Korea, so we both knew what to expect. Amateur boxing tournaments are difficult, because given a bad draw and an off day you can be out in the early rounds. In a way it's a bit easier when you get to the final stage, when you can focus on one man and concentrate all your attention on him,' says Lennox.

'I'd thought I was better mentally prepared than Bowe. In an earlier round I'd helped him beat a Russian. I'd fought the guy a year before and I knew how to handle him. I said. "Just go out there and hit him with the left hook," and passed on other stuff I'd learned about him. But Bowe couldn't seem to concentrate on what I was saying. He wasn't focussed. I knew then he lacked a bit of determination, he wasn't mentally there.'

For anyone expecting instant fireworks, the first round of the final was a disappointment. Lennox can be a slow starter, and the opening minute crept by at a snail's pace. He was too cautious at the start, and allowed Bowe the initiative. Bowe ducked his head into Lewis's side, and worked on the body. It was an untidy round, and Lennox was tagged by three solid right upper-cuts. 'Waking-up punches', he called them later, but one of them bloodied his nose.

Lennox fought his way out of the jam and escaped further punishment. Then things started to go wrong for the American when he picked up a public warning at the end of the first session for using his head dangerously.

'I was going for his body and he caught me with an upper-cut, which was his best punch,' says Lennox. 'It gave me a bloody nose, and I was upset with myself at getting caught by a sucker punch like that.

'When he hit me, I threw a hook to take his head off. But it missed. But it did snap me awake. I thought, "Yeah, all right. I'm going to have to try a little harder, and I won't get suckered into that upper-cut again."'

Waiting in Lennox's corner was an angry coach. 'I had to shake him up a bit,' says Teodorescu. 'He definitely won the round, but he still stayed too much with Bowe. I shouted at him, "What the hell are you doing? Let's go out and fight him and knock him out. Stay away and throw your long right hand. Use your natural skill. Don't start slugging."'

The roasting roused Lennox out of his torpor. He rushed out of his corner and Bowe was in trouble from the bell. The first standing eight count came after a series of five punches – a left, another left, and then a quick right–left–right combination – sent Riddick leaning back over the ropes and gasping for air like a beached whale.

The end came after 43 seconds of the round, when another looping right and then a fast left rocked Bowe again. Another eight count and it was over.

Bowe protested that he was fit to continue, waving his arms at the ref. 'The decision to stop the fight was somewhat premature,' he complained later. 'I was trying to indicate I was OK.' But he complained to no avail – the medal already belonged to Lennox, who, not surprisingly, saw the fight differently. 'I really tagged him,' he said. 'His eyes were glazed and he was gone.'

'I wish I'd knocked him cold, because he's complained ever since that he was robbed. But he was gone. He was walking around trying to waste time so that he could get his sense back. His eyes weren't there, so the referee gave him the count. One more punch and he would have been out of it and he'd have had no grounds for complaining about anything.'

At the decision there a dizzying outburst of joy in the winner's corner. Teodorescu lifted the giant boxer as high as he could manage without giving himself a double hernia. Lennox broke free and sashayed around the ring, arms held high in victory, a smile as wide as a Cadillac grille, his maple-leaf vest looking like the man wearing it – pristine and unruffled. The dream that had sustained him through all the bad times had at last come true. After seven days of recriminations brought on by the Johnson affair, Canada at last had a clean and clear-cut victory to celebrate.

'There was this tremendous explosion of all sorts of emotions in me. Joy. Gratitude. A sense that all the trials and tribulations had been worth it. I realized that this was a moment Muhammad Ali and other great men had achieved, and I was grateful to have arrived at that pinnacle like them,' he says.

He was hustled from the ring by two Canadian officials. 'They were really tense,' he says. 'They were in a big panic because of the drugs issue. They kept shouting to me, "Don't touch anybody's hands. Don't drink anything." I don't think they relaxed until I'd given a sample and it was safely sealed up.'

Back home, in the living-room of her apartment on West Mount Road in Kitchener, his mother Violet nearly missed her son's great moment. In fact the whole of Canada nearly missed the fight – CBC didn't begin airing the bout until well into the first round. One minute they were doing a profile on Lennox, then they suddenly switched late to the action from Korea. If Lennox had been a bit more urgent with his big bombs no one at home would have seen them as they were delivered.

In West Mount Road Violet faced the box with family friends – Glen Nicely, Beverley Alfred, and Wilfrid Phillips – all of them shouting encouragement at the screen. 'We couldn't hear the commentary, but that didn't matter because it was so clear that Lennox was winning,' she says

Violet should have been at the ringside in Korea right then. She had booked her holiday to coincide with the games, arranged a flight, and got ringside tickets. But then a fork-lift truck ran into her at the factory where she worked. The accident broke her right foot in four places, and the break had to be pleated. Now she was in plaster, on crutches, and under doctor's orders not to get too excited.

'We were watching the TV and the TV cameras were watching us, because they were making a film of us as we watched the fight. Everybody was there. The noise was really deafening. When Lennox won, it was the happiest moment of my life. I was still in plaster up to my knee and I was still in pain from my operation, but when he won I forgot all about the pain and the plaster and I jumped up from the couch and danced around the room. My foot is still bad – even now I can't wear proper shoes – but when he won I was so excited I was dancing.'

The phone started ringing, as it would through the next twenty-four hours, as friends queued on the line to congratulate the winner's mum. On the edge of the sofa, Glen Nicely was in ecstasy over the scenes coming live from Seoul. He sat transfixed by the screen, shouting 'Yes' at the television. He shouted 'Yes' seventeen times.

Then as the anthem 'O Canada, our Home and Native Land' filled the room and the gold medal was placed around Lennox's neck, the magnitude of her son's achievement hit Violet with a flood of emotion. She broke down and cried. 'Praise God,' she said.

Lennox held a small Canadian flag and a bouquet of flowers as the large Maple Leaf was raised behind him. 'As the flag went up and I looked straight ahead into the distance', he says, 'it was a strange feeling after all the years of waiting for that moment. Inside I was excited and happy for all my friends who had wanted me to win so much. But outside I must have appeared as calm and cool as an iceberg. I was in a blank state, thinking, "I've achieved it. What else is there? Is this it?" '

On the victory podium, Riddick Bowe asked Lennox if he could stand beside him on the highest step. Lewis responded with a laugh. 'He wanted to know if he could share the limelight with me. I told him, "That's only for one guy." Then, as we shook hands and stepped down, he said, "See you in the pros." '

8

Cunning Like a Fox

The dream of signing a good young heavyweight is the soothing draught that small-time managers lull themselves to sleep with: a panacea against wakefulness and cold winter nights. There are desperate men out there who would shave a Kodiak bear and put it in the ring if they could pass it off as a raw young hopeful. Damon Runyon had it about right: 'A fight manager may have a lightweight champion of the world, but he will get more heated up about some sausage who scarcely knows how to hold his hands up if he's a heavyweight.'

A share in a good young heavyweight means serious money – like breaking the bank at Monte Carlo, or being the only sober man in a poker game. Which is why every four years the power-gamers in boxing attend the Olympic Games. They know the surest way to eliminate the glorious uncertainty involved in finding a good prospect is to pick your man straight from the winning rostrum after the medal ceremony.

Tyrell Biggs, the Olympic super-heavyweight champion in 1984, said, 'This is the college of boxing. The kind of degree you get depends on how far you go. If you win the Olympics, you get a doctorate.' It's a doctorate that brings a fat fee with it if you choose to turn professional.

In the boxing hall at any Olympics, the winners are generally surrounded by a clucking entourage of men anxious to do deals. Fill in your favourite descriptions of Don King, shake, and dilute to taste, and that's what it's like. The movers and the shakers in the fight game react to gold like sharks in a feeding frenzy.

When he stepped down from the rostrum, Lennox may have thought the world was his oyster. But the men behind Mallet were convinced that Lennox was solidly theirs. After the medals ceremony at Seoul there was no feeding frenzy among the managers, agents and promoters. American operators were there by the dozen, but none of them got to Lennox. When scouts for the major professional boxing organizations approached Adrian Teodorescu, he told them they were wasting their time – his heavyweight was already taken. He nailed them with Mallet.

'Everybody you spoke to, from the fighters to the trainers, seemed to say, "Don't touch them. They've got a whole group behind them,"' says promoter Stan Hoffman of the Houston Boxing Association, who was at the tournament in Korea.

On the long plane journey home to Toronto, Lennox mapped out his future. 'In the past the gold medal meant money. So I thought some money might come my way,' he says. 'I thought the telephone would be busy with people making offers.' At the last Olympics, when he had not even made the semis, there had been an offer of $500,000 (Canadian) to turn pro. How many zero's would be bid this time?

But a Niagara of lucrative approaches did not engulf him. By the time he got home to Canada, all the American players in the game had assumed he had gone ahead and signed a deal with Teodorescu, Hurst and Mallet Sports Inc.

Two days after returning from Seoul, still elated by victory but a little jet-lagged, Lewis was given a contract by Mallet. It was a standard boxing agreement, with a 65–35 split of income (with Lewis to get the larger share). Lewis's debt wasn't mentioned; neither was the signing bonus.

Lennox was disgusted when he was told the bonus would be

1 The conquering hero. Lennox enjoys his victory over Derek Williams in 1991.
(© *Allsport/John Gichigi*)

2 Violet Lewis in Forest Gate, newly arrived from Port Antonio, Jamaica.

3 Lennox's first passport photograph, aged six.

4 Jackson Five lookalike. Elder brother Dennis, aged eight.

5 Lennox, newly arrived in Canada, aged twelve.

6 The class of '79 at Margaret Avenue Senior School, Kitchener, Ontario. Lennox, in the back row, was fourteen.

7 The young athlete hard at work.

8 Caveman Lennox in 1985.

9 Blowing out the candles on his seventeenth birthday.

10 In at the deep end. Lennox in the Dominican Republic to box at the Pan American Games.

11 Roadwork around the suburban streets of Kitchener.

12 The Cameron Heights football squad. Lewis (34) was dazzling in the brief time he played high school football. Courtney Shand, now his fitness trainer, is number 35.

$25,000. 'I thought it was an insult, to be truthful,' he says. 'When they offered me that tiny sum I said to myself, "Holy smokes, man." I looked at the medal and said, "This really didn't mean nothing." Lots of managers and promoters had offered me more than that to turn professional when I hadn't got the Olympic gold.'

Meanwhile Adrian Teodorescu had been busy. According to Ontario government records, on 5 October 1988 – three days after Lennox won his gold medal – Teodorescu became a director of Mallet Sports Inc. One day after that he was appointed the company's president. He had always planned to be central to the outfit's operations, picking up an annual salary of $100,000 as head coach of Mallet's team of boxers, as well as receiving a percentage of each fighter's earnings, plus his director's fees.

'It would have been a windfall for him. He'd have been paid three ways,' says Lennox. 'He'd have been coach, manager and president – picking up money for every title. At no stage earlier on did we realize that he'd be the president. Everything was really hush-hush and secretive.

'When we got back from the Olympics, Egerton [who won a silver medal at middleweight in Korea, having boxed three bouts with a broken hand] and I couldn't believe what was happening to us. I suppose we were disappointed more than angry, because we'd both trusted Adrian.

'We'd both entered the loan agreement. We thought the payment date was for a year later – 31 May 1989 – but they said it was 31 May 1988. That was only six weeks after we'd signed the papers and we were not able to pay back any money then, because we weren't earning any money. We had no income apart from grants and loans. At that stage all our time was taken up with training for the Olympics.

'Thinking about it, it does seem that this was pressure on us to sign a pro deal with them after the Olympics. They may have thought we'd be so worried about the so-called debts we owed them that we'd cave in, because that was the only way to get the debts forgiven.

'We were under constant pressure from Teodorescu to sign up with him and Mallet, but we dug our toes in and said no. We had the feeling we were being railroaded and they were trying to take advantage of us.

'There was a lot of pressure, but I'm very strong-minded. I believe we create our own stress. If it's a situation you can't do anything about, then you shouldn't worry about it.'

Teodorescu saw each boxer separately. When Lennox refused the deal, he was asked not to tell Marcus about his decision. 'It disappointed me, because all three of us had been so close. It seemed to me that he was playing us off against each other. I was shocked. In his way perhaps he meant good. But the deal wasn't in our interests,' says Lennox.

'I never talked to him after that. I bet if you went to his gym my picture would be there on his wall, but I've turned myself off from him like a switch. He was so close to me, we shared a special moment at the Olympics, then he tried to do a sharp deal. I was really disappointed. He hurt me, so I switched myself off from him completely.'

When both boxers baulked at the contracts offered them, Mallet got heavy, sending them itemized accounts of what the company claimed the medal-winners owed it. Lennox was billed for $169,778.99. Egerton Marcus got a bill for $115,000.

The detailed accounts make intriguing reading. Under the terms of the deal, Mallet could use its discretion in paying whatever expenses it felt necessary to allow Lewis and Marcus to 'maintain both a reasonable quality of life and advancement in [their] boxing endeavours.' Just how liberally this was applied was shown by the fact that Lennox was billed for Mr Teodorescu's flight to South Korea, for some of Mr Teodorescu's clothing and $3,000 for a press party in his honour after winning the gold medal.

John Hornewer, now Lewis's attorney, has little time for

Teodorescu. 'What he was saying was, "If you want to go turn pro somewhere else, you've got to pay us back the advance plus the penalty of $100,000."

'They really tried to put a lot of pressure on Lennox and Egerton to make good on those agreements. It just got very petty and ugly, because, with all fairness, Adrian had led the financial backers to believe he had control of these guys and could deliver them. When it became apparent that they weren't satisfied with what they were being offered after the Olympics, and they thought it was unfair, that grip started to loosen.

'Once I found out about the agreement, I tried to talk to the Mallet people about how we thought it wouldn't stand up in law. They were kind of desperate to have it validated, just to have their investment returned to them, plus something – but preferably having a boxer sign with them.

'I don't think Lennox ever really knew what he signed. He just signed because that's what he felt he had to do at the time. Yeah, he remembers signing. He remembers being in the room with Adrian and Hurst, and Hurst's accountant. He remembers signing it. But I think he just relied on Adrian and said, "If this is what we've got to do, this is what we've got to do" – not knowing that Adrian had set this thing up for Adrian's future much more than for Lennox's or Egerton's future.'

Adrian Teodorescu has been a fighter all his life. He boxed at various weights and classes from the age of eleven. He had 250 bouts as a junior and 156 fights as a senior, mostly at middleweight, losing only 26. He was a professor at the Constanta Institute of Physical Education in Romania, and has coached boxing teams at every Olympiad but one since 1964. (He wasn't in Los Angeles in 1984 because he'd only recently arrived in Canada from Romania.)

At fifty he still looks in good condition – a tough, chunky man, with a moustache and strands of hair combed Bobby-Charlton-style over his balding dome. There is something eerie about his conviction that he was doing the best for his boxers and not trying to grab control of their bandwagon. He is a man possessed by overflowing sincerity who says he's still hurt at what he feels was a kind of betrayal by Lennox.

'I don't understand how he could change so much in those post-Olympic times. I was like a father for him, and all of a sudden after the Olympics he changed. I don't know what kind of influence he had from the outside. Lennox was a very loyal person, and then he changed.

'I don't know what word or reason made him be so rude and rough. If I am loyal to somebody, I'll be loyal to the end.'

He maintains that without the financial support from David Hurst Lennox would never have won his Olympic gold. 'Without Mallet, I am telling you, we wouldn't have been able to achieve anything. Mallet was the company that came behind us – financially and more. We got a great moral support from them.

'I have no words to describe David Hurst's attitude. He was a real friend. All the garbage that came in the press after and all the words, whoever started it had a very bad intention. They were trying to change Lennox's and Egerton's attitude towards us.

'Mallet provided them with money before the Olympics so they could train, with the idea that afterwards they would turn professional. But this gentleman [Hurst], he didn't want to make any money with us. He just wanted to have a good time and fun with us, to be around us. He didn't need money – he was retired at the age of forty-four.'

He claims the pre-Olympic deal with Mallet was an insurance against defeat in Korea. 'I said, "Look, guys, it's good to have something in writing so that after the Olympics it doesn't matter what the results are." You take a chance going into the Olympics, because you can be out in the first round. Accidents can happen. A bad day and you are out. So I wanted to have something solid for them after the Olympics.'

He claims that Lennox's initial signing-on fee would have been £100,000. Subsequently this was raised to $250,000, with an offer of 25 per cent of the company.

'The critical newspaper reports did not understand the situation,' he insists. 'They thought that Dave Hurst and the others were just sharks who saw they had a chance to do something with Lennox. But it was far from that. The percentage they were going to take from Lennox was simple peanuts.'

'As long as I was involved they were not asked to pay back any money. Dave Hurst never mentioned to me that he asked the kids to pay back the money they'd used to support themselves. When I talked with him after the articles appeared in the Toronto papers, he said, "Adrian, I don't want even to hear about this garbage." I never asked. Maybe his lawyer did something, I don't know.'

According to Teodorescu, John Hornewer, Lewis's lawyer, was initially called up from Chigaco to work for Mallet. 'John took a very strong stand against Mallet, when actually he was supposed to be hired by Mallet,' Teodorescu says. 'Very strange things happened. With any other promoter or manager they were getting two bullets in the head if they didn't sign after all this company did for them.

'You know, it's upsetting, because you spend a lot of time and you spend a lot of money. Really, Dave was a gentleman. He never argued or asked anything from us. He came forward and gave us all the support. He was acting more like a friend than a boss.'

After the adverse publicity, Boxing Ontario suspended the coach and held an investigation. 'I needed Lennox to come and speak up in front of this committee on my behalf,' says Teodorescu. 'I asked his mother to ask him to come. And I got very upset because he had no respect to call me back and ask what it was about. He didn't come, so that really hit me straight in the heart. I couldn't believe it – he was more than my son.'

In May 1989, after a tribunal of Boxing Ontario officials had met for three hours, the coach was cleared of any conflict of interest involved in signing the boxers for Mallet while they were amateurs. A published list of expenses indicated that Teodorescu had been receiving £1,200 a month from Mallet before the Olympics. But he claimed at the tribunal, 'I was not taking money for coaching, but acting as a pipeline and passing the money on to other coaches who helped to train Lennox.' (The other coaches were never named.)

After the hearing he said, 'I'm happy, but then again I'm not happy. After all I did for these fighters, and for Canada, I don't think I deserved what I had to go through in the last few weeks.'

The tribunal was a formality, he says now: 'It couldn't do anything to me because this company Mallet didn't move from the ground – it wasn't an active company. The company was just a piece of paper, and my title was "President" on that paper.'

'The Romanians are very sentimental – we put a lot of soul into things. I wouldn't work with anybody if I didn't like them, or if he doesn't match my blood. So, after the relationship I had with Lennox, I am very disappointed the way things turned out. I have to emphasize, before the Olympics Lennox was like more than my son. I even neglect my family to go with him and take care of him.

'When people talk to me about Lennox, I say, "I can't tell you too much about professional boxer Lennox, all I can talk about is Lennox to the Olympics. Sure I wish him to be a great fighter. If he wants it or not, his name will always be linked with mine because of the Olympics. I can always say I was in his corner that great day.'

Context is important: five years on everyone has had time to rehearse their lines and edit their version of events. Time is capable of altering or distorting the picture. But one thing is clear about 1988: at the Olympics everything was fine between Lewis and his coach, then suddenly it wasn't. When he got home, Lennox felt Mallet was trying to strong-arm him into a contract, and he resisted. Adrian Teodorescu, for his part, still feels he was hard done by.

David Hurst now spends his time mostly in Florida. 'I think we lost a great friend and a good friend for boxing,' says Teodorescu. 'I was passing him all my ideas to develop here a great stable of professional boxers. At the same time we wanted to build up a Palace of Boxing here in Toronto for all people. I wanted to continue working with amateurs, as young people are the grass roots of boxing.'

He may have missed out on his Palace of Boxing, but since then Teodorescu has set up a stable of professionals at his Atlas Gym near Toronto Airport. It's run along the lines he tried to pioneer with Mallet. His squad of a dozen fighters includes some who have come through the Olympics, including the white heavyweight prospect Tom Glesby, who boxed for Canada at Barcelona. 'Maybe one day Tom will be heavyweight champion,' he says. 'I like to think so.'

Maybe the last word ought to go to Arnie Boehm, who was close to both men. 'I worked well with Adrian. I respected him and his knowledge. But I can see through his front now. He wanted to be like Don King. Adrian foresaw a golden opportunity. All my kids, he makes them sign on the dotted line. "It's for your benefit." For *his* benefit. He thought they were stupid, those kids. But like old Hock McComb used to say about Lennox, "People think Junior's dumb, but he's cunning like a fox." '

9

What's it Going to Take?

Outside the ring, boxing can be as cruel as it is in it. The true business precept in the sport is straight out of *Martin Chuzzlewit*: 'Do other men, for they would do you.'

Boxing negotiators have been, traditionally, men like Doc Kearns, the remarkable manager of Jack Dempsey. who was not above cheating and conniving to get his man the best deal. In ruthless pursuit of the $300,000 purse for the Dempsey–Tommy Gibbons fight in Shelby, Montana, in 1923, he harried citizens of the cattle town into insolvency.

When the locals offered a part payment of 50,000 sheep in lieu of money, he declined. 'What the hell would I do with 50,000 sheep in a New York apartment?' he said. In his later years he was fond of telling how Dempsey and he – but mostly he – broke four Montana banks.

Things have become less piratical since the 1920s, but only marginally so. The eccentric commercial morality that currently exists is probably best captured in the story told by American sports commentator Bob Waters. 'I was talking with Bob Arum [a promoter]. He told me something and I said, "But Bob, yesterday you told me the exact opposite." "I know," Arum answered. "Today I'm telling the truth. Yesterday I was lying."'

When new boys come face to face with the thrusting entrepreneurs and the me-first ethic of the boxing business, you would expect them to end up like the hapless citizens of Shelby – wiser, but poorer. Which is why the making of the deal which launched Lennox Lewis as a professional boxer is all the more remarkable. It was undertaken by a fresh-faced young lawyer, John Hornewer, then twenty-eight, while he was doing a master's degree in business studies at North Western University, near Chicago.

His professors gave him permission to fly around the United States with the heavyweight and to use the negotiation of Lewis's contract for professional status as a practical extension of his studies. Hornewer proved himself a good student: he ended up with his MBA, and the job as lawyer to Lennox Lewis. His client won a profitable contract with the Roger Levitt Group that set him on the road to becoming heavyweight champion of the world, and a millionaire.

Hornewer had always been a boxing buff. While studying law at the University of Illinois, and, on graduation from there, when working briefly in the tax department of the Arthur Andersen accounting firm, he had kept up his childhood interest in the sport. A college friend had gone to university in Las Vegas, and John used to travel to Nevada in the spring breaks to see the big fights in the casinos. There he met Don King, Larry Holmes and other stars in the boxing firmament.

His other hobby, photography, got him prime ringside spots at a dozen title fights. Subsequently he gave some action shots to a young Canadian fighter, Matthew Hilton, who, when he learned Hornewer was a lawyer, used him to negotiate the contracts for a couple of his fights.

When the Mallett Group thought it had netted Lewis and Marcus after the Seoul Olympics, Hornewer was called up to Toronto in October with a view to becoming involved in the Mallet set-up. Lennox warmed to him immediately. He says, 'He was rumbustious and energetic. A small man, but not afraid to shout as well.'

He didn't like what he saw. 'It was too disjointed and there were too many fingers in the pot,' he says. 'To me it seemed that Adrian [Teodorescu] was going from the amateurs to the professionals, and the people behind him with the money had no experience in boxing. It just seemed like pie in the sky. Just from meeting him I wasn't confident in Adrian.'

After that first meeting with Lennox, he was convinced that Mallet's strategy for turning him from an Olympic gold-medal-winner into a well-rewarded professional was flawed.

'There were a lot of people who – how shall I say? – were the usual group of suspects who come around successful athletes when they are looking to turn pro,' he says. 'They're saying, "I can do this for you", "I can do that for you," "Just sign a contract and I will do this for you". There was Adrian. There was a guy named Kingsley Bailey, who was claiming to be a public-relations person, who suddenly turned up from out of the blue.

'Lennox is the kind of person who just lets people hang about, and, as long as it's not costing him anything, they are just around. When we discussed my working with Lennox, I told him I would work with him without a contract. If I could deliver what I said I could – which would be to introduce him to everybody in boxing and find the best deal for him – then I would be paid to do that job. If I couldn't do that, then all my expenses were down to me and he would not lose out. That was the approach Lennox seemed to take with everyone: if you want the chance to work with me, you're on your own to produce results.'

Lennox and Hornewer did not meet again until December. In the meantime, as the wrangle with Mallet and Adrian Teodorescu continued, Lennox was fêted.

Four years previously, before he went to the Los Angeles Olympics, CBC television had conducted a poll in Kitchener to find out how well known Lennox was there. Ninety per cent of the people questioned had never heard of him.

It was all so different after Seoul. The boy nobody knew was given the keys of the city by Kitchener's mayor, Dom Cardillo, who declared that 10 October 1988 would be Lennox Lewis Day. Now everybody was shouting his name. Firetrucks with their sirens wailing escorted his open-topped limousine to City Hall past a sea of Canadian flags and a large sign in golden letters saying, 'Congratulations Lennox'. As his car edged its way through Market Square, the crowd hemmed it in. It seemed as though they all wanted to touch him. When at last he got to a microphone and held his medal aloft, Lennox shouted, 'I'd like to thank the entire community. This gold is for you.' The home-town folks went wild.

Under the headline 'Hometown Hero', a leader in the local paper, *The Record*, said that Lennox had proved 'one need not be a brawler or a loudmouth to be rated with the world's best boxers.'

It went on:

That rating is bound to open doors when the 23-year-old Cameron Heights collegiate grad launches his professional boxing career sometime soon. It will also, no doubt, attract some folks claiming long-standing association with Lewis even though they couldn't remember his name before.

Neither is likely to unsettle the new champion whose natural calm has often misled the 'experts' into doubting his hunger to win. These doubts should now be dispelled.

Seoul for Lewis was an end – and a beginning. He proved the power of his lefts and rights, administered with an intelligent and an almost elegant effectiveness that could yet make him one of the classic stylists of the boxing ring.

After he won his gold medal, Air Canada offered Lennox a free air ticket anywhere in the world. He passed it on to his older brother, Dennis, and invited him to fly from London to Canada, join the celebrations, and stay with him in his apartment in Toronto.

'It was very generous of him,' says Dennis. 'Most people would have used the ticket for themselves.' Dennis took a couple of weeks off from his job as a salesman at Just Leather, a furniture shop in Wembley, and his younger brother showed him the sights in Toronto.

'The people really celebrated his medal in Kitchener, but the general atmosphere in Canada was fairly low-key. I think the Ben Johnson affair put a bit of a dampener on the achievements of all the other medal-winners.

'I couldn't help feeling that somehow Lennox wasn't being given the full credit for his gold medal,' says Dennis. 'There were several people around him who seem to be more like hangers-on than working for him. I was a salesman, and I'd been a DJ and a ticket tout. I've always been a good talker. Selling is my profession. I was a bit disappointed to see that there Lennox was with a gold medal, everybody was talking about him, and yet he had no endorsements, no sponsorship, no nothing.

'I don't care what anyone else says about this, but I was the first one to suggest that Lennox should come over and base himself in England. I told him, "Why don't you come to England? There's only Frank Bruno there. Everyone's hungry for a really good heavyweight." He didn't say much, but I think I planted a seed of an idea in his mind.'

But there were a lot of people anxious to arrange his professional baptism in Canada. A Kitchener business triumvirate of Bob Neufeld (he of the abortive moneymaking schemes to support Lennox before the games), and two car dealers, Dennis Schlueter and Gary Stockie, set up Emerald Power Group Inc. to launch Lewis's pro career. Their aim was to provide Lennox with financial guidance while protecting him from 'all outside people and influences'.

As chairman of the four-man executive committee and a 60 per cent shareholder in a corporation worth $1.5 million (twenty-five non-voting shares at $60,000 dollars apiece), Lennox would have had complete power of veto. That was fine, except that the triumvirate of local worthies would have owned 40 per cent of the voting shares and that worked out at $200,000 apiece. Lennox couldn't live with that. He also wanted a signing bonus.

'Bob Neufeld called me to find out what I intended to do,' Lewis says. 'I just told him that the contract wasn't for me – it was more for them. When I first met him he came across as a very nice man, but I was less impressed as time went on. I don't think he quite realized that I had my wits about me.'

'He'd have been dealing in strength through the corporation,' claimed Neufeld. 'It was a gilt-edged opportunity for him. We wanted to ensure his future. He'd have been laughing.'

Another local deal had ended in bitterness. Lennox's adviser Kingsley Bailey had told newspapers the Emerald Power offer was a joke. There was an echo in all this of *The Record*'s leader-column warning to Lennox about people with an eye to the main chance. Neufeld and Bailey had accused each other of being opportunist, and Neufeld told Lennox that unless he got rid of Bailey the deal was off.

Kingsley Bailey was at that time a lodger in Lennox's Toronto apartment. In return for food and lodging, Bailey, whom Lennox had known from his boyhood in Kitchener, took phone messages when Lewis was away and made appointments for him.

'Kingsley was a bit of a ducker and diver who was a very smooth talker. He answered the phone and took messages, and got a place to stay in return, so in a way we were both helping each other out. But then he started calling himself my press officer,' says Lennox.

'He was always on at me to write down on a piece of paper a job description saying he was my press officer, but I told him I couldn't do that. Then I found out that he was harming my name with people. Some people wouldn't deal with me because Kingsley wanted to make himself part of the deal as well. People didn't want him because they didn't like him.

'So I told him he'd have to find another place to stay. I came home one day and he was just gone. I didn't hear any more from him until I'd turned professional and was doing well – then he started trying to sue me.'

In Toronto they still tell the story of how boxing promoter Irving

Ungerman, who made his fortune in the chicken business, tried to lure Lennox into his stable after the Olympics. The chicken magnate's team had once included heavyweight contender George Chuvalo. (It was Chuvalo who in 1979 boasted, 'I'm the best heavyweight fighter in Canada, and I'll still be the best when I'm dead seven years.')

Lewis listened attentively, and then noted that Ungerman was also guiding the career of Donovan Boucher, a black welterweight who had ended the career of white hope Shawn O'Sullivan. 'Mr Ungerman,' Lennox observed with the utmost courtesy, 'you managed Donovan Boucher, who made all those chicken commercials for Swiss Chalet, and you sell the chickens to Swiss Chalet. So now how come Donovan Boucher isn't making any commercials?' For once the garrulous Ungerman was lost for words.

By now the Americans were becoming aware that no deals had been struck with the Olympic champion in Canada. One of boxing's most highly respected promoters, Dave Wolf of New York City, who took Ray 'Boom-Boom' Mancini to the WBA lightweight title, began talks with Lennox about his professional future.

In November 1988 Lennox attended the Sugar Ray Leonard–Donny 'Golden Boy' Lalonde fight at Caesar's Palace in Las Vegas to talk to Wolf. There were links there – Lalonde (who lost his light-heavyweight title to Leonard) was born in Kitchener, and he and Lewis had trained together at the Waterloo Regional Police Boxing Association – and Lennox was tempted.

Next came an invitation from Lou Duva and Shelly Finkel of Main Event – who controlled Evander Holyfield, the then cruiserweight champion of the world – for Lennox to go down to their gym in Norfolk, Virginia. This immediately rang alarm bells with his lawyer, Hornewer.

'I was still on the outside looking in,' he says. 'I got a phone call from Jim Tait, who was Lennox's mother's lawyer. He told me that Lennox was going on this trip to Main Event's training camp. My advice to them was to make sure that he didn't hit anything. I said, "If he breaks his hand, or injures himself, what good is he?" I told them that he was an Olympic gold-medallist and he didn't need to prove anything to these people.

'Actually Lennox went down to the camp and did nothing for a week. He just sat there and watched, and the Duvas were really upset. A few weeks later when I ran into Lou Duva, the father, he had a really great quote. He said to me, "That Lennox Lewis came down to Virginia. We wanted to check him out. He comes down like he's trying to check us out. How dare he?"

'Lou Duva told me that lawyers were ruining the business, and I had to point out to him that his son Dan, the promoter, is a lawyer.'

By now three months had passed since Lennox had won his medal, and still no deal had been struck. 'At the start I felt pressured,' says Lennox. 'I didn't want to make a wrong move. That's why I took so long to chose the right deal.'

But Hornewer geed him up. 'Lennox and I had a number of conversations, and I said, "Look, you have to get yourself out. You've done nothing, no one's coming your way – you've got to let yourself be known." So we prepared some kind of press kit and we mailed it out to people with tapes of Lennox in action.

'When Lennox and I sat down together and agreed to work together, we had an understanding. I said we would listen to every offer from anywhere and decide on what was the best offer for him. It was not always going to mean the most money. He agreed, because I think that's something that he and Arnie Boehm had discussed all his life.'

For all his relative inexperience, Hornewer was not daunted by the task ahead. 'I'd had some experience working with the boxer Matthew Hilton, so getting Lennox a professional contract wasn't as difficult as it sounds. What you have to do is treat it as a business project. Luckily I was in business school – the best in the country – and my professors allowed me to shift my courses and go for it. They wanted me to use this experience as part of my coursework. So I was applying everything that North Western could offer to the Lennox Lewis proposition.'

The lawyer and the boxer decided to fly down to Las Vegas at the end of January 1989, just after Lennox had been awarded the Order of Canada medal. They were accompanied by the Lewis family attorney, Jim Tait. The gambling city was the venue of the Frank Bruno–Mike Tyson heavyweight title match. The two big men were due to fight at the Hilton Hotel on 25 February, and for the whole month the place was like a noisy, bustling boxing convention.

It was obvious to everyone in town that Hornewer was hawking Lewis around, trying to match him with the highest bidder. Cedric Kushner, the bulky, walrus-moustached South African promoter, wisecracked to Honrewer, 'Even Ray Charles can see you're shopping this kid around. What's it going to take to get him?'

'What's it going to take?' was the question on many lips. Bob Arum, Emmanuel Steward of the Kronk Gym in Detroit and the Duvas were all interested in signing Lewis. So were the people behind Frank Bruno – Mickey Duff and Jarvis Astaire. Stan Hoffman of the Houston Boxing Association had even drawn up a provisional contract for Lewis and Hornewer to sign.

'I wasn't ten steps into Caesar's Palace when Mickey Duff called me over,' recalls Hornewer. 'He said to me, "What's it going to take? Just tell me – no bullshit. What's it going to take to sign this boy?" I said I really didn't know – that we were just in town to hear what people had to say to us.

'Everybody's line was that they couldn't get into a bidding war over Lennox. I told them to make their best offer, then we'd make our choice, and left it at that.'

Later, Duff and Jarvis Astaire treated Lennox and Hornewer to an expensive dinner at Caesar's Palace. Lennox says, 'I never really spoke – John did the talking. I just sat there eating and listening. I was just seeing what kind of people they were. Mickey Duff was trying to talk us out of a signing bonus, as he didn't want to give us any money.

The dinner with Mickey ended, but it was clear he still wasn't interested in paying a signing bonus. Now, four years later, he'll be kicking himself.'

Hornewer knew that in Lennox he had an attractive, highly saleable piece of merchandise. 'Our advantage was that we had something they all wanted,' he says. 'Lennox was a rich commodity, because he'd won the gold medal at the Olympics. When he beat Riddick Bowe, the favourite for the top medal, it made everybody in boxing sit up and take notice. But, more than that, he was tall and good-looking. He had a pleasant personality. He was articulate and friendly. In addition, he came from a respectable background – there was no criminal record or ghetto delinquency to spoil the picture. In terms of all his pluses he was a marketing man's dream.'

But, oddly, the first man to make a positive move to secure the services of Lennox Lewis wasn't a boxing promoter or manager. He was a British press photographer – Lawrence Lustig, of the tabloid *Daily Star*.

That February two other British champions as well as Bruno were due to fight for world titles in America. Lloyd Honeyghan was to defend his welterweight title against Marlon Starling, and Dennis Andries was to meet Tony Willis in Tucson for the light-heavyweight championship. That meant that Las Vegas was a seething mass of British newspapermen who, on slow news days, were all looking for extra stories that would justify the expense of them spending a month in the gambling capital of the world.

On the morning of 4 February, Lustig was sitting in the foyer of Caesar's Palace waiting to attend the press conference that would announce the upcoming Sugar Ray Leonard–Thomas Hearns rematch.

At thirty-six, Lustig has spent most of his career travelling the world taking pictures at the ringside of the top boxing events. He went to school in the East End with Charlie Magri, a former world flyweight champion, and was best man at his wedding. Although he never boxed seriously himself ('I sparred a few times with Charlie. Or rather Charlie hit me a few times'), Lustig is a keen student of the sport and has an encyclopaedic knowledge of all its faces.

He had seen Lennox box as an amateur at the Commonwealth Games in 1986, and at the recent Seoul Olympics, but for a moment his memory let him down and he couldn't place the face sitting opposite him.

'This very big, very good-looking young black fellow was sitting on his own reading a newspaper,' he recalls. 'I kept on thinking, "I know you. Who are you?" Then suddenly it clicked that I had seen him at the Olympics. I walked across and introduced myself, and he seemed quite startled that anyone should recognize him.'

Lustig remembered that Lewis had been born in the East End of London, and saw the germ of a story there. They agreed to meet later in the day, when Lustig would take some photographs and Lewis would be interviewed by Lustig's colleague, Ken Gorman.

'I asked Lennox, since he was British-born, whether he'd been in contact with any British promoters or managers. He said he'd spoken to several people, but wasn't very optimistic about anything coming of it. I told him, "There are other people," and mentioned Frank Maloney, who at that time was promoting with Terry Marsh under the banner of Ambrose Mendy's World Sports Corporation.

'Lennox hadn't heard of any of them. So I said, "Have you heard of Nigel Benn?" He said, "Oh yes – my brother Dennis has told me about him. He's the young middleweight who's been knocking everyone out. They say he's a mini Mike Tyson." I told Lennox and John Hornewer that obviously Maloney and Mendy were eager to get a foothold into big-time boxing. I offered to make a phone call and introduce them, and they said, "Go ahead."'

'The idea of launching my professional career in Britain appealed to me straight away,' says Lennox. 'At that time I had it at the back of my mind that I would sign with Stan Hoffman and HBA, because he was such a nice, open man. Then, when Lawrence started mentioning other managers and promoters in England who might be interested, it reminded me of what Dennis had been telling me. I knew how eager British fans were to have a really good heavyweight champion. It suddenly struck a chord. I was born in Britain. Why couldn't that boxer be me?

'I was getting a bit tired of going round America visiting their boxing people without them making a really good offer to me, so I said to John, "OK, let's give these people a try."'

That night, at midnight in Las Vegas, Lustig rang Ambrose Mendy at home. It was around eight on Friday morning in London, and Mendy had already left for work. Lustig rang his office in Tower Bridge Road, where at five past eight Maloney was already at his desk and picked up the phone.

'Basically Frank's reaction was "Fuck off!",' says Lustig. 'I said to him, "Frank, you're not going to believe this, but I've just spoken to the person I believe will be Britain's first heavyweight champion since Bob Fitzsimmons." Frank, being Frank, said, "Have you been on the piss?" I told him, "Frank, you know I don't drink. I've been speaking to these guys, and they're looking for management. When I told him a bit more, Frank started to get very excited and kept saying, "Let me talk to them, let me talk to them." I told him it was gone midnight and they were probably in bed, so we arranged it that I would get them to ring him at the same time the next morning.'

The following midnight (eight o'clock on Saturday morning in London), Lennox and John Hornewer came to Lustig's room at the Flamingo Hilton and he put in a second call to Maloney. The 15-minute long-distance call led to the deal that would make Lewis a British-based boxer, and Frank Maloney a big-time manager.

'I don't think Frank has ever actually thanked me for that introduction,' says Lustig. 'I know he's grateful, but I don't think he's ever actually put his arm around me and said, "Thanks." But there again he's never hidden the fact that I was the person who introduced him to Lennox, and in a friendship you don't really expect people to keep saying "Thank you" all the time.'

10

Write Your Own Contract

Frank Maloney gunned down the M25 in his white Mercedes 190 on the morning of Sunday 23 April 1989, hoping there were no police lurking on those raised ambush spots on the hard shoulder. He was tense. He hadn't eaten properly for twelve weeks, and he'd hardly slept the night before.

His thirteen-year-old daughter Emma was in the front passenger seat, but for all the notice he took of her she might as well have not been there. He ignored both Emma and the speed limit as he pressed the accelerator pedal to the floor.

He couldn't get to Gatwick Airport fast enough. He was speeding to meet Lennox Lewis, who was jetting in from Toronto to sign a deal with The Levitt Group that would make Maloney Lewis's manager.

Since negotiations had begun in February, Maloney had lost 16 lb. in weight. A born worrier with a queasy stomach, he had been off regular meals for most of that time, surviving on a diet of ice-cream and puddings.

Life is sometimes overdone and usually very corny, but this really was a fairy story. A small-time operator – a little guy who had spent most of his time on the outer fringes of boxing – was about to pull off the biggest deal of his life. As the speedometer hovered at around the ton, Frank worried. He had never quite made it to the big league. He was a small-hall promoter who looked after mostly ham-and-egg fighters. Now he wore the kind of fretful expression which said he feared that even at the fifty-ninth minute of the eleventh hour there might still be a sad ending to the fairy story.

'I was just like a big kid I was so excited,' he recalls. 'The deal was almost there, but I was still worried in case something went wrong and he wouldn't sign. I was like a schoolboy on the morning of a big exam – all jitters and nerves. I couldn't wait to get to the airport so I could reassure myself that Lennox still wanted the deal to go ahead.'

It was eighty-six days since Lawrence Lustig had phone Frank from Las Vegas to tell him Lennox was ripe to be persuaded to turn professional in Britain. 'When Lawrence rang me, I said, "How do I get in touch with this Lewis? And, if I do, why should he and his attorney take any notice? They're not going to want to know someone like me – small, struggling to establish myself." He told me I knew my way around and ought to put a package together.'

After his first talk with Hornewer, Maloney spent hours on the phone trying to contact him in Chicago. In one twenty-four-hour period he rang fifteen times. 'The first time I phoned, his mother was quite polite to me,' he says, 'The second time I phoned, she said, "I've given him your message. He's not back." The third time, she said, "Do you ever sleep?" It turned out it was two o'clock in the morning in Chicago. I told her I was sorry but it was very important that I got in touch with John.'

After a dozen more calls, Maloney finally tracked down Hornewer. He offered him and Lennox first-class fights to Britain and accommodation at the Churchill Hotel in Portman Square so they could fly to London to discuss a contract. 'At the time I didn't have any backers. Nothing. But I had met a couple of people from The Levitt Group and I was sure they'd be as excited about Lennox as I was. From the very start I had an optimistic feeling about the whole idea. I thought Lennox would be very good for British boxing and that I could look after his career better than anyone else. The adrenalin really was pumping away. I felt maybe the tide was going in my direction at last.'

Frank Maloney is a busy, Napoleonic little man who shares with the French emperor a lack of inches, a flinty ambition and a nervous stomach. He was born forty years ago in the Elephant and Castle, a tough working-class district south of Waterloo Station, the eldest of three sons of a building worker from Tipperary.

His accent is heavy with the pie-and-eels atmosphere of South London, and he has the curriculum vitae to go with it. It is so colourful it could be the work of a low-life fiction writer with his imagination in overdrive.

At the age of fourteen Frank was sent to the Liverpool seminary of the Mill Hill Fathers to train to be a missionary priest. He lasted a little over a month. During a retreat, he bunked over the wall to purchase a bulk order of sweets which he tried to flog to his fellow seminarians. The father superior told Frank's dad, Tom, that perhaps his son's missionary zeal would be better accommodated outside the priesthood.

Then Frank was despatched to Epsom, to train to become a jockey. His stay there was even briefer than with the Mill Hill Fathers. 'Being a stable lad was too much like slave labour for my liking,' he says. As a teenager he ran a Sunday bric-à-brac and secondhand-furniture stall in East Lane market with his brother Eugene. Then in turn he worked as a chef, as the catering manager at the Inland Revenue offices at Somerset House, as an East End publican and as a part-time trainer and boxing promoter.

He had always liked sport, though his cock-sparrow size – 5 feet 3½ inches – was an anchor to his ambitions. At football he was a winger who had a trial for Wimbledon. 'I was very fast, but I used to get shoved a lot.'

He was an even better boxer. 'I started scrapping at the Sacred Heart School in Camberwell. I was the smallest kid there, and my mum [Maureen] kept me in short trousers. She was always telling me, "You'll grow up soon enough, Frank." Because of those short trousers I always got a lot of mick taken out of me, and reacted.'

He had sixty-four bouts as an amateur flyweight (8 st. to 8 st. 6 lb.). He contemplated turning professional, and had a few pro fights goes, but his heart was never really in it. 'I went to the professional gym where John Conteh and all them trained. I watched how some of the fighters were getting misused, sparring with the good guys and treated like nothing more than pieces of meat for them. I was horrified. I thought, "I'm not letting them do this to me."

'I was amazed at how these fighters got treated. They were like slaves. They used to tell me how much they were earning – sometimes as little as £60 or £70 a fight. I felt that none of the people cared about their fighters unless they were going to be champions and earn them some money. I thought to myself that, if I got involved in professional boxing, I would never let that happen. If I became a manager, I'd make sure that none of my fighters were treated like meat.'

Maloney became an assistant to many of the leading faces in the game. He was a trainer with Frank Warren, a matchmaker with Mickey Duff, and a mostly small-hall promoter with parvenus like Ambrose Mendy and Terry Marsh. When Marsh, the former world lightweight champion, met him he was surprised by his cherubic looks. 'I remember being impressed by Frank's youthfulness,' he said. 'I thought all boxing managers were aged about fifty, and I didn't realize you didn't have to be middle-aged to be a businessman.'

Frank is unequivocal about the ruthlessness of his trade. His general views of the game are set down in the book *Lord of the Rings*. He told Harry Lansdown and Alex Spillius, 'People in boxing are hypocrites, and they will suck your blood dry. Socially I keep myself aloof from people in boxing. I have been turned over so many times. I'll work with anyone, but it's pure business. Loyalty doesn't exist in boxing.'

As for negotiating business deals, 'Boxing is all about bluffing,' he says. 'It's like poker, whoever has got the calmest nerve will win. That's what it boils down to. You bluff in business don't you? It's a matter of how much nerve you've got. How much you can sell yourself. You have to sell yourself to the people you're raising money from, you have to sell yourself to TV, then the fighter has to sell himself to the public. It's about selling all the way down the line.'

But Frank had never been short of big ideas to get him out of the small time. The trouble was that not all of them worked. He once brought over Roberto Duran, the former welterweight champion, to spar a series of exhibitions with Frank's brother Eugene. On another occasion he signed up a Colombian lightweight named Juan Arroyo. Maloney flew him in from Miami and gave him the catchy *nom de guerre* 'The Baby-Faced Assassin'. The nickname proved too close to the truth. After losing his only British fight, the pock-marked Arroyo was sent down back home for thirty years for a variety of crimes involving menaces.

To set up his latest big idea, Frank first met Charles Meaden, the old-Harrovian head of Olympic Gold (later called Levitt Sports and Entertainment). This was the sports-management subsidiary of The Levitt Group, which employed stars of the calibre of Seb Coe, the Olympic-gold-medal athlete; John Hollins, the footballer and former manager of Chelsea; and Jimmy Lindley, the ex-jockey and BBC racing commentator.

At the time, Roger Levitt had ambitions to compete with IMG – Mark McCormack's giant sports agency – and was attempting to gather to his company leading players in football, boxing, polo, golf, the turf, and grand-prix motor racing. 'I told Charles about Lennox Lewis and said if we could put together a package and sign him they could open up their own bank and make themselves the biggest sports management company,' says Maloney.

Meaden, a jovial and balding thirty-eight-year-old, had boxed at Harrow but had never ever seen a professional fight. Novice though he was in the sweet science, he didn't need much persuading that Lewis would be a major capture for The Levitt Group. 'The thing that really attracted us was the fact that Lennox was actually British,' he says. 'To have someone of that talent who was actually British was very exciting.'

The day Lennox and John Hornewer arrived at Heathrow, Maloney could meet them only briefly because he was flying out to Belfast within the hour with a middleweight, Anthony Logan, who was to fight that evening on a Barney Eastwood bill in the Six Counties.

Frank waited at the arrivals barrier in Terminal Three for Lennox to arrive from Toronto, and spotted him as soon as he walked through the automatic door from customs. 'Straight away I knew it was him, because he was so huge – head and shoulders above the other arrivals. As he came through, I introduced myself and he put a massive arm around me. I looked into his face and just saw the look of a born winner there. I thought to myself, "This man knows where he's going and what he's looking for." He had destiny written in his face, and I thought, "With God on my side, if only I could be lucky enough to put all this together."

'I had a feeling that fate had kept him from signing with anyone else in the three months since he'd won the Olympic medal, and that somehow I'd been chosen.'

The deal he proposed would ally the boxer with a major financial group which would treat the potential champion like a blue-chip investment, ploughing in money to launch his professional career in the hope of a lucrative dividend when he became world champion.

'The Levitt deal we had planned would be a big breakthrough for boxing – something that had never quite been done before in this country,' says Maloney. 'If only we could persuade Lennox to base himself over here it would certainly be a coup of Britain.'

And a coup for Maloney too, of course. But he couldn't talk business immediately, because he had to fly to Belfast. 'All the time I was in Belfast I couldn't think of anything else,' he says. 'All I wanted was to get straight back to England to start doing the deal.' Frank's charge, the unfortunate Logan, was knocked out in round two by Victor Cordova, and next day Frank was on the first flight back to Heathrow.

Lennox and Hornewer were taken to the Churchill Hotel and provided with two minders, Alan Matthews and Brian Homer. 'Lennox and I were paranoid,' says Hornewer. 'We thought, "Gee, who are these two guys?" The minders were telling us that they were there to make sure we didn't talk to Mickey Duff, Frank Warren or Barry Hearn, because The Levitt Group had paid for our trip.'

'When we got to our rooms, we checked them for bugs – looking behind pictures and under lamps. We thought that if these people were going to the extent of giving us minders then we must be bugged,' says Lennox. 'These guys had a room right down the hall, and were taking turns to stand in front of our door. We thought they were crazy.'

In fact Lennox got on well with the minders, and, apart from business, the visit turned into a bit of a tourist jaunt. 'We did a few typical tourist things and had fish and chips and went to the East End,' says Lennox. 'I met up with Dennis again, and we had a good time. That's how we looked at it in a way. Even if the deal came to nothing, we'd had a pleasant trip to London out of it.'

Hornewer did ring Mickey Duff – not to do a deal over the boxer, but to get a ringside seat for the Duke McKenzie–Tony DeLuca IBF flyweight title fight at the Albert Hall on 9 March. He had a commission to take photographs for *The Ring* magazine. During the fight, he got involved in an elbowing match with the *Daily Express* photographer Jack Kay. The British press photographers were still resentful about the bad positions they had been allocated in Las Vegas for the recent Bruno–Tyson fight. (As Kay commented at the time, 'I'm here to cover the first Briton fighting for the heavyweight title in America for thirty years, and I'm stuck on the fucking Arizona border.')

While Hornewer and Kay jostled each other, across the ring the *Daily Star* photographer Lawrence Lustig, who had introduced the American to Frank Maloney, pretended not to know who he was. 'Everyone was saying, "Who is that blankety-blank American?" I didn't let on, because I knew that John was over here negotiating with

Frank Maloney and I didn't want to give the game away.'

The early talks with The Levitt Group were simple. 'They basically said, "You write your own contract. You tell us what you want." We took them at their word and went home and did just that,' says Hornewer.

Before they flew home, Hornewer and Lewis sensed that The Levitt Group was easing Ambrose Mendy out of the picture. 'It seemed at the time they were kind of pushing him away,' says Hornewer. 'Ambrose said to me one day in a hallway, "You can ask whatever you want, and don't be shy" — and I certainly took that into consideration when we went back home. I could tell, though, he was being pushed out because they weren't comfortable with Ambrose because of his reputation. He had the whole brat-pack mentality with Nigel Benn and a bunch of other black athletes whom Ambrose was representing.

'The image that Roger Levitt wanted to portray was of this dyed-in-the-wool conservative firm that wasn't involved with people like Ambrose. So, even though Levitt spent some money sponsoring Mendy fights to get the Levitt name out there, I never believed they wanted anything to do with Ambrose officially. Frank Maloney was their man.'

Maloney had still only ever seen Lennox box on video, but the more he saw of Lewis on that first visit, the more he was impressed by him. 'There was an aura about him,' he says. 'Whenever he went into a room, people felt his presence. It wasn't a cocky arrogance, like some boxers — more a quiet self-confidence which said, "I'm Lennox Lewis, and I'm confident in anything I do."

'The history of the Olympics shows that most heavyweight and super-heavyweight gold-medallists turn professional and do well — a lot of them going on to win world titles. But there was an air of extra authority about Lennox. I knew that if he was guided right and managed right he'd get there. I thought to myself that if I couldn't steer this man to the top then I didn't deserve to be in this business.'

The boxer's first view of Maloney was equally favourable. 'He seemed to say what he meant, with no nonsense. He was straight to the point and honest. There wasn't anything underhand about him,' says Lennox. 'He seemed full of enthusiasm for the project – 100 per cent behind my career – and I liked that.'

Over the next ten weeks there was a series of meetings in Britain and America to iron out the deal. Stories that Maloney was on the verge of pulling off a startling coup were beginning to circulate, and jealous rivals made attempts to poison Hornewer's ear with lurid allegations about Frank.

'When some people realized that I was beginning to look like a serious player and that I might pull off the deal, John started to receive certain phone calls regarding my behaviour, my background. A number of things were said: that I was a shady person and I ran around with certain characters. At one stage – before it came out that the Levitt Group was backing me – they even intimated that the money could come from the drugs trade. They were implying that I was some sort of gangster, when I haven't even got one conviction.'

Who made those calls? Maloney thinks he knows, but, the laws of libel being what they are, he chooses to take the Fifth Amendment. 'You have to be very careful how you word these things, don't you?' he says.

Another obstacle in the way of a quick and satisfactory deal was the attitude of a couple of directors in The Levitt Group. 'One of my main worries was the attitude of a couple of the directors there who wanted to get on to the bandwagon,' says Maloney. 'They were people who knew nothing about boxing but just wanted to be close to the boxing action, like groupies or star-gazers.'

The first time he met Roger Levitt, Maloney voiced his complaints. 'I was sitting in The Levitt Group offices one day when everybody started tidying up their desks. I asked what was going on, and they said Roger Levitt was coming on to the floor. I'd never seen Roger Levitt at that time, and I said, "What's that got to do with the spring-clean?" They told me, "He's like God."

'Anyway, this guy appeared in my doorway with a big cigar in his hand, wearing an overcoat with a fur collar. He looked at me and said, "Who are you?" and I told him. I knew who he was anyway, but I said, "Excuse me asking, but who are you?"

'He said, "I'm Roger Levitt, the owner of the company. And you're supposed to be the man who's running my boxing, getting me this heavyweight."

'I said, "Yes, but a couple of your guys keep messing it up, so we may lose out on it." So then he said, "We heard you're good at what you do – prove you're good. Get that signature on the contract at all costs. If you have to get on a plane tonight, get on one. Remember, I don't take no for an answer." '

So Frank flew to New York – only his second visit to the USA – for more meetings with Lennox and his lawyer. The Levitt Group had booked them into a down-market hotel, The Milford Plaza. Frank stayed on there but moved the boxer and Hornewer into the best suite at The Marriott Hotel.

'The Milford was a transit place,' says Maloney – 'really rough. It didn't matter to me, staying there, but the rooms were so small Lennox could hardly move around in his. Whenever I drive up 42nd Street now I laugh at the place.' (The next time The Levitt Group had to find rooms for the Lewis team in New York, for the press conference to announce that Lennox was turning professional, they were all booked into The Ritz.)

Over the next couple of days, the men argued their way towards a final deal. It was to astound the boxing world, establishing a high market value and giving decision-making powers to a boxer who had yet to prove himself in the hostile environment of the professional ring.

It gave Lennox a six-figure signing-on fee of around £150,000, the use of a house in Bexley Heath, Kent, a company Mercedes, a gold watch, living expenses of £500 a week, a £15,000 annual retainer for

John Hornewer, and even a place for his mother, Violet, on the Levitt payroll. It would split the boxing revenues 70–30 over the five years of the contract, but would also cover training expenses and pay the salaries of Lewis's training team. The company would provide £750,000 in health and life insurance policies, and make provision for education and training when Lennox retired. A sum was also set aside to cover any outstanding debts in Canada.

Even with all those perks, Lennox would retain control of the big decisions in his career. He would be able to veto the choice of trainers and opponents, and he would retain the right to fight for other promoters if Levitt did not come up with matches that met with his approval.

It was a revolutionary contract which would alarm some people in boxing. When Stan Hoffman of the Houston Boxing Association was made privy to its contents, he told Hornewer, 'If anybody in boxing sees this contract it'll ruin the sport. You cannot give boxers such a good deal and this much say.'

'I know of no other contract like it,' says Hornewer. 'To me it was a fair deal for a human being. It was trying to get a safeguard to give Lennox a nice head start in his boxing career. But if things didn't go as well as we'd hoped he'd be protected on the downside by at least having a commitment to educating him for the future if his boxing career didn't work out.

'But the most important thing in it was giving the boxer himself the control and say-so on the big decisions in his career. Most times boxers are treated as commodities who are told what to do and when and who they are going to fight. In Lennox's case the final word is always with him, and will always be with him. This is not slavery – these people were working for Lennox Lewis and not the other way around.'

'All boxers are used,' says Lennox. 'I realized that I would be used during my professional career, because so many people have to take their cut of the money a boxer earns. But I only wanted to be used to a certain extent. I wanted to make sure that I retained a clearly defined percentage of whatever I earned, and that I had control over my own destiny.

'There are too many boxers who go through their careers being told what to do and who to box, and they end up badly off. There are too many fighters who are left like Marlon Brando in *On the Waterfront*, thinking about what might have been.

'I was determined that it wouldn't happen to me. I've studied what happened to some of the great heavyweights like Ali and Joe Louis. What dragged some of the greatest men in boxing down were drugs, drink, bad managers, bad financial advisers, hangers-on, bad fights, bad health and bad women. I was determined that none of these things was going to happen to me.

'I wanted to leave boxing with my finances secure, my brains intact, and no gold-digging female honing in on me because of what I'd earned, not because of what I'm like.'

One of Maloney's main selling-points was the impact Lewis would make in Britain if he was successful. 'I said to them, "Look at the marvellous reaction there was when Frank Bruno came back from fighting Mike Tyson – and he was a loser. I asked them to imagine what the reaction would be if we produce a world heavyweight champion. Lennox would be crowned king of England.'

He didn't have to sell too hard: Lewis and Hornewer already knew about the likely public reaction from the taxi-drivers who had ferried them around London on their first visit. 'When John and I came to Britain to talk about the deal, we realized how much people wanted a heavyweight on the scene that would give them a bit of pride,' says Lennox. 'People were hungry for success, because for a hundred years we hadn't had any. I thought if I could supply a bit of success that would be great. If I could actually win a world title, the impact would be unbelievable.'

Maloney was quite happy with Lewis having the major influence on the direction of his career. 'He wanted to have a big say, and I was always in favour of that. In some cases the boxers have been no more than sweated labour for the manager, but I've never wanted that,' says Frank.

'I tell a young fighter when he signs with me that now he is a professional, he is in business. I don't tell him we're going to have a father-and-son relationship, because that's crazy. What we've got is a business relationship where we work together as partners. If the boxer takes a larger share of the earnings, then he's entitled to a larger say-so in what happens to him.'

The deal The Levitt Group had offered Lennox was the sweetest inducement most people in boxing could ever remember, yet that didn't stop Frank fretting away every motorway mile as he drove from Crayford to Gatwick to meet the boxer. He needn't have worried. Lewis arrived with hardly any i's to dot or t's to cross, and the next day in Levitt's headquarters he duly signed the contract that made Maloney his manager.

'At the start, I didn't seriously think I'd get Lennox', Maloney says. 'I mean, let's face it, every manager in the world was after him, and when I made the first approach it was almost tongue-in-cheek. I just kept on at him. Lennox says what he liked about me in the end was I wouldn't take no for an answer.'

Six weeks earlier Mickey Duff had scoffed at Maloney's efforts to sign Lewis. In a taxi ride to the Phoenix Apollo Restaurant in Stratford, London, where they were going to finalize details for the Watson–Benn fight, Duff had said to him, 'Oh, so you're trying to sign Lennox Lewis. You won't get much joy there.' Maloney had replied, 'I think I've got as much chance as you, Mickey.'

Maloney's doggedness had won through. In boxing the unexpected sometimes does happen and a man from the undercard beats a top-liner.

13 An early bout. Lennox (note the lack of biceps) is coached by cornerman Arnie Boehm.

14 An early international win over a young Swede.

15 Training in the Catskills with seventeen-year-old Mike Tyson. Left to right: Kevin Rooney, Lennox, Cus D'Amato, Arnie, Mike Tyson.

16 Lennox wins his first Canadian senior Championship by beating Vernon Linklater.

17 Sparring as an amateur with Donovan 'Razor' Ruddock.

18 Desperadoes. Arnie and Lennox on the Wild West Coast, in Los Angeles for the 1984 Olympic Games.

19 The North American Championships in 1987. Left to right: Arnie, Lennox, Adrian Teodorescu, Asif Dar and Egerton Marcus.

20 Lennox presents his Olympic medal to his mum in 1988. (© *Kitchener-Waterloo Record*)

21 Running on the beach at Hilton Head, South Carolina, for the Tony Tucker fight. Left to right: Courtney Shand, Lennox, Eugene Maloney.

22 Sweating it out in the gym with Courtney Shand. In the background are Pepe Correa, trainer, and Frank Maloney, manager.

23 The first pro fight in Kitchener. Lennox celebrates a TKO over Greg Gorrell in five rounds.

24 Lennox boxes Razor Ruddock into a corner in October 1992. (© *Allsport/Holly Stein*)

25 The King of the Ring. Lennox makes an impression on Tony Tucker in Las Vegas in May 1993. (© *Allsport/John Gichigi*)

26 The winning corner. Manager Frank Maloney punches the air after Lennox's win against Tony Tucker.

11

Enter Roger Rabbit

The trouble with Roger Levitt, generally speaking, is that he is generally speaking. The smooth-talking supersalesman is so loquacious that members of The Levitt Group, behind his back, used to call him Roger Rabbit. 'The thing with Levitt', says Frank Maloney, with typical cockney bluntness, 'is that he never really said anything. He just talked.'

But Levitt's golden stream of verbosity proved mesmerizing to financial institutions in the 1980s. By himself in 1989 he earned more than £5 million in insurance and pensions commissions. His advisory company which provided financial services to the rich and famous was one of the biggest in the country – worth, he claimed, £150 million before his empire crashed on 13 December 1990 with debts of £40 million.

After a public-school education at Wellingborough and a brief period as a Marks & Spencer salesman, Levitt started selling life insurance and pensions for large companies. He branched out on his own in the mid-1970s, when initially many clients were customers of his father's wholesale clothing business. Soon his charisma, determination and enthusiasm had won him big clients, generating commissions of at least £200,000 in a single year. One of his biggest deals was to sell an £11 million single-premium bond investment to the then Blue Arrow chairman, Tony Berry. The commission on that sale alone was over £500,000.

Dapper and charming, he is hand-crafted from the best traditional city-magnate materials, wearing pin-striped suits and Technicolor bow-ties, and smoking huge Davidoff cigars. At the peak of his success he seemed to know the answer to virtually everything. Whether he was talking about his beloved Arsenal Football Club, selling an insurance policy or promoting grandiose schemes, Levitt projected dynamic confidence, engulfing his listeners in a tidal wave of pep.

In spite of all his undeniable qualities, there is, though, an unendearing slickness about him which his demeanour does not help. He looks like a stealthy iguana with a Groucho Marx moustache, giving the distinct impression that his smarm content has risen above government safety levels.

When The Levitt Group was riding high, most of his lieutenants fawned around him like the courtiers of a benevolent despot. But there was always a healthy nonconformity among the men in his boxing subsidiary, who were unimpressed by his magisterial gab. Amending the remark that Dennis Rappaport once made about the American boxer Ray 'Boom-Boom' Mancini, they used to say, 'If bullshit was poetry, Roger's last name would be Shakespeare.'

Levitt had always been a sports fan. His company had an executive box at Arsenal's Highbury Stadium, and also sponsored Barnet, then a non-League side. He also ran a Levitt polo team, which beat Kerry Packer's expensively assembled outfit in 1989. Boxing was another passion. His father, Ben, took him to the ringside to see his first professional fight at the age of four, and he remembers being held aloft in the arms of Freddie Mills, the world light-heavyweight champion in 1948. 'My father boxed for the army when he did his military service during the Second World War,' he says, 'so you could say that boxing is in my blood.'

His boxing division – Frank Maloney Promotions – was just one of many subsidiaries within The Levitt Group. He once described it as his 'rich man's pastime' which 'took up just 4 per cent of my working day'. Under Charles Meaden, the Group's sports section involved big names like jockeys Steve Cauthen and Pat Eddery, and England footballer Paul Parker. The idea was to manage stars while they were active in their sporting careers, and secure their futures by investing their earnings in pension schemes. But the signing of Lennox Lewis in April 1989 put Levitt in the newspaper headlines, where he enjoyed basking, and soon the development of the boxer's career took priority over his other sporting interests.

'Roger Levitt just wanted the Lennox deal because he loved collecting athletes,' says John Hornewer. 'They were like toys to him.' Charles Meaden echoes this view: 'Levitt wasn't involved in the day-to-day planning of Lewis's career. He simply signed the cheques. What he really enjoyed was the high-profile side of the venture – flying in executive aircraft to see the fights, that sort of thing.'

There are a number of stories that illustrate Levitt's flamboyant style. When Lennox fought his fourth professional fight, against Steve Gerber of Bradford at the City Hall, Hull, on 10 October 1989, the private flight bringing Levitt and his guests to Humberside was late.

The hall was packed. The fights on the undercard had come and gone, yet five minutes before the first bell in the Lewis fight it looked as though the prospect's backers might not make it.

The preliminaries dragged on. There was some unrest at the delay. Even as Lennox was introduced as holder of the Olympic super-heavyweight gold, six ringside seats remained manifestly empty.

Then in the nick of time and a swirl of cigar smoke the VIPs filed to their places. If they had been a couple of minutes later they would have missed all the action and their costly aerial dash would have been pointless, for it took Lewis only 90 seconds to send the sacrificial offering spinning out of control in a tangle of limbs on to the canvas.

Satisfied with the buoyancy of his investment, Levitt had seen enough. As Gerber was helped back to his corner, the Levitt entourage jumped up and hurried for the exit. Chauffeured cars to the airport meant they could be back in London almost before their prized asset had time to shower and put his civilian clothes back on.

After that fight, the American-based boxing promoter Cedric Kushner was summoned to a meeting at Levitt's West End headquarters at Devonshire House, 1 Devonshire Place. Kushner has been around the block a few times in his colourful career. When he emigrated to Europe from South Africa at the age of twenty, he worked his passage on a cargo boat by cleaning out the cages of some zoo-bound rhinoceroses. He went on to work as a pool attendant at the Fontainebleau Hotel in Miami Beach, to scalp tickets at the Munich Olympics, and to make a fortune in the States as a rock promoter. Later he gravitated to boxing promotion, controlling the likes of Tony Tucker and Gerrie Coetzee.

A larger-than-life character himself, Kushner, then aged forty, thought he was immune to the eccentricities of boxing, but he wasn't prepared for his extraordinary meeting with Levitt.

'It was quite odd,' he says. 'I was ushered into this very elegant boardroom. Levitt was at the end of a long table surrounded by acolytes, all identically dressed in business suits, who nodded in unison when he spoke and laughed obediently when he was being funny. They were the embodiment of the term "yes-men".

'He addressed me for about half an hour. I could hardly get a word in edgeways. It was almost mesmeric – a cross between Mussolini and Walter Mitty.

'Lennox had just had his fourth professional fight. He was a very good prospect, but he still had a lot to learn. Already, though, Levitt was talking about celebrating his fortieth birthday by booking the New Orleans Sugar Dome for the first defence of Lennox's heavyweight title.

'He had great presence. When he spoke he made you believe what he said, even though you may have thought it was absurd. I've been at some strange meetings during my time in boxing, but this whole scene was bizarre. I remained cordial and civil, even though it was an absolute waste of time from A to Z. In the end, I told him that maybe he was being a trifle premature and perhaps we could have dinner some time. I haven't seen him since.'

Striking boardroom vignettes like that illustrate merely the hubris before nemesis. Behind its lavish front Levitt's company was in disarray. On 11 December 11 1990 The Levitt Group went into liquidation. Two days later the chairman was arrested at his mansion near Highgate golf-course and charged with the theft of £665,000. After his arrest, his lawyers mounted an emergency action and he was declared bankrupt.

Levitt is due to appear in court on 1 November 1993, and in the intervening three years the charges against him have been whittled down. Now, with four co-defendants, he denies just one charge of fraudulent trading contrary to section 458 of the Companies Act. The Lennox Lewis contract was one of the assets realized by the liquidator from KPMG Peat Marwick McLintock.

While not as ebullient as he once was, Levitt still has high hopes of rebuilding his business and boxing interests. In his office in Dorset Street, sitting under a large signed photograph of Lennox Lewis in action, Roger Levitt says that, although his business relationship with the champion is now severed, the friendship of Lennox has been a comfort to him, his wife, Diana, and his five children since the crash of his company.

'Certainly he's given me a lot of strength – and I him – over the last three years,' he says. 'I hope, please God, after the end of my court case that I return to boxing and will once again know him, and be closer to him.

'It has been the privilege and the pleasure of my life, for both myself, my children and my wife, to share in the making of the first British heavyweight champion of the world this century. I feel very strongly that, had it not been for good fortune, good timing and my company's money, Lennox Lewis might never have made it.

'I am proud, and will be proud to my last day, that I was the man who took him from the Olympics, brought him back for Britain, and set him on the road to the current success he enjoys.'

Levitt was Lennox's paymaster for his first fourteen professional fights. The last contest he enjoyed before his company went under saw Lewis win his first title when he stopped the European heavy-weight champion Jean-Maurice Chanet in six rounds at the National Sports Centre, Crystal Palace, on 31 October 1990. The twenty-month involvement cost The Levitt Group £1.25 million according to its ex-chairman. 'For that period there was no money in it for The Levitt Group. It was all one-way traffic,' he says.

But he has no regrets about spending a fortune only to miss out on the financial rewards that come with owning a share in a world champion. 'As long as I'm associated with him as a friend, which I am now, my reward is quite fine,' he says. 'I never look back on money. Money is something that comes and goes. I've never placed a tall order on money for money's sake. It's what you can do to help your family and help other people – that to me is what the creation of wealth is all about.'

He says he followed Lennox's progress through the Seoul Olympics on television in 1988 and was immediately excited by the idea of bringing him to Britain to start his professional career. 'I was obviously over the moon about the whole thing,' he says. 'I suppose I was a little bit too easy, too philanthropic, too benevolent. But I agreed to what in the end turned out to be a very generous contract.

'I wasn't just throwing gifts or money at the young man. I felt that if he had an environment to grow in that would make him feel secure, mentally and financially, he'd be able to box in a more relaxed fashion.

'By and large the majority of boxers never quite seem to make as much money out of it as they should. If they are unfortunate not to get to a world champion's position, they can have a fairly mundane financial reward, having put in the best years of their sporting life and not benefited from it. I was determined if I was going to be associated with a young man of Lennox Lewis's calibre I was going to make sure he got the rewards early in his career. I wanted him to feel totally comfortable and concentrate on boxing and not worry about the very next penny.

'In my business, which has a lot to do with body language and inner strength, you can see people and visualize their capabilities. I knew from day one that he would be world champion.

'I was very much his mentor in terms of how his career was going to go. I can remember distinctly where Frank Maloney and others weren't sure in the early days that he would get to be world champion. I had no doubts from his very first fight that he would be. I told him so from day one, and I always used to call him "Champ".'

When his court case is resolved, Levitt intends to go back into business and boxing ownership. 'I hope to be at the next Olympics, in 1996. I shall be there bidding correctly for new talent at all weight levels. Unlike some British boxing managements, I'd be prepared to pay the price to give the boxer a fair deal, as I did with Lennox Lewis – perhaps even a generous deal to help the young man, whoever he may be, to go forward.

'Now of course the great assumption I'm making is that by 1996 I'll be in the position of making enough money to bid. But – if you're a betting man – I'm not bad in a photo finish.'

His office is like a grotto to the rich and famous people he has met. Apart from the Lennox Lewis and Arsenal memorabilia, he displays pictures of himself posing with royalty and politicians. There is even an old Christmas card from the Prince and Princess of Wales on display. It is as though he reinforces his worth by showing that a whole host of dignitaries and celebrities are his bosom friends.

It is genuinely touching when he recalls a Sabbath eve when he and his family lit the candles over a meal with the boxer. 'It was just a wonderful feeling. I felt that all the effort we had put into his career and future was beginning to really shine,' he says. 'It sounds a little bit poetic, but looking at the candles and listening to him – and seeing my family – was a wonderful warm feeling, because he is a very exciting young man with a good heart. He was absolutely 100 per cent part of my family.'

12

Cecil B. De Mille
in Reverse

American managers deride the approach of their British counterparts by saying that they can build good fight records but they cannot build good fighters.

They have a point. It has become a habit over here to groom our young heavyweights by pitting them against a collection of imported has-beens, never-weres, stumblebums, Mexican road sweepers and ring-worn remnants from the Zimmer-frame section of obscure American gyms.

The prospects quickly run up a series of victories that look good on paper. They move up the ratings as their unbeaten record earns them publicity and a following. But, come the inescapable day when they are matched against genuine opposition, they generally end up out-manouevred, out-gunned and horizontal. They are not so much being groomed and tested as potential champions as being hyped towards a big pay-day.

In contrast, young fighters in the USA are given a more rigorous schooling. They fight more often, against sterner opposition, and learn their craft thoroughly along the way. Dennis Andries, the Guyana-born former world light-heavyweight champion is a case in point. When he was based in Britain he looked like an untutored novice who would always be an also-ran. Transported to the Kronk Gym in Detroit, under Emanuel Steward, where he learned his business and gained confidence from high-quality sparring, his improvement was almost miraculous.

Planning the professional debut of Lennox Lewis, Frank Maloney was faced with a dilemma. He did not want to bring his boxer along too fast. An early set-back against a hard man, a convincing beating from an opponent who was too wily for him, might erode the luminous confidence that is vital in a budding champion. On the other hand, he didn't want to stand accused of feeding the Olympic gold-medallist inept bums (though he was accused of this anyway).

'I'd sat down and studied Frank Bruno's record. He had gone twenty-one fights as a hero, winning them all on stoppages. Then he'd got knocked out by a nobody – Bonecrusher Smith, who at that time wasn't an established name. I was certain that this wasn't going to happen to Lennox. We were going to take him to the grass roots. We didn't want to give him pushover fights, because he would learn nothing that way, but we didn't want to push him too fast. We wanted him to take his time adapting from the amateur ranks to the professional game, learning how to pace himself over longer fights and getting to know how to cope with different boxing styles and types of opponent.

'I could have put Lennox in with Bruno on day one and he would have whipped him. That's my honest belief. He could have taken the British title with his first fight – that's how good he was. But what opponents could we have found after that? They would have all gone to ground. And, remember, Lennox was still untried as a professional. We needed to give him a few tests and set him some posers to solve before we put him in with the really top-class guys.'

Amateur boxing and professional boxing are so different they could almost be different sports. It's like trying to compare camp-fire cooking with a six-course banquet prepared by the Roux brothers. However good an amateur champion is, his professional trainer almost has to strip his skills down to basics and start again.

Lennox's mum, Violet, had insisted that her son should have an

American trainer. Her favoured option was that Lennox should join the Kronk stable of Emanuel Steward. Now, while conceding that Lennox would be based in Britain, she still insisted that an American should be hired to impart some of the tricks of the trade that can only be learned in Stateside gyms.

On his trip to New York, Maloney had had talks with Angelo Dundee, the legendary trainer of Muhammad Ali, with a view to him overseeing Lennox's professional debut. Talks broke down, however, over the percentage Dundee wanted for his involvement and his reluctance to base himself in Britain for long periods. In his place, the man The Levitt Group finally chose was a tough ex-marine from Plainfield, New Jersey, six years in the Corps, called John Davenport. He was the choice of John Hornewer, and was appointed against the advice of Frank Maloney.

Another man in the running had been Teddy Atlas, Mike Tyson's trainer in the amateur ranks, but he was eventually ruled out. 'I met him,' Lennox says, 'but there were strong rumours that he once pulled a gun on Tyson. He had a bad rep, so we decided not to go with him.'

As for Davenport, his testy attitude was to cause problems in the months to come. 'The only thing I thought was in John Davenport's favour was that he was a disciplinarian,' says Maloney. 'He seemed quite a stern fellow. Other than that, his record had nothing. The enquiries that I made were that he wasn't the greatest trainer. I wasn't 100 per cent for Davenport from day one. But John Hornewer seemed to want him and pushed for him, and Lennox accepted him.

'But I knew Lennox would outgrow Davenport. Everyone knows my relationship with John Davenport was never smooth. It was an up-and-down sort of association, because I knew John wasn't the right trainer for Lennox Lewis. All he wanted around were yes-men all the time, and he was anti everything to do with the English.'

The uneasy alliance lasted until after Lennox's nineteenth fight, against Levi Billups at Caesar's Palace, Las Vegas, on 1 February

1992. Against the awkward Billups, Lennox was taken ten rounds for the first time before winning a clear points victory. But Lennox was unhappy with the atmosphere in his training camp, and Maloney decided to let Davenport go.

The boxer's first meeting with Davenport in the Catskill Mountains in upstate New York was amicable enough, though, and the camp settled down to six weeks of hard training before the debut fight, in London, on 27 June 1989. After the first week, however, the feisty trainer from New Jersey was almost ready to pack his bags.

'I would say that after a week I was ready to throw up my hands, quit, and go home. The reason for that is that he had a European style – that stand-up-straight style – which from my experience I know doesn't work in the professional ranks. I didn't think he was going to be able to make the necessary adjustments, and I was ready to call it a day,' says Davenport.

'One thing that I admired in him, though, is that he's a remarkable athlete. He had tremendous litheness, strength and athleticism. What stopped me from quitting is that he's a very fast learner. Once an idea kicks in, he picks it up very easily. After that first difficult week, everything I showed him he just picked up straight away.'

As far as Davenport is concerned, amateur boxing is more like pat-a-cake than fighting. 'The amateurs have the white portion of the glove which you have to hit the man with,' he says. 'It's all about scoring points. With the professionals it's all about power and knocking people out.

'Lennox had been coached at the Olympics by a Romanian. And you could tell, because he had an upright, European style. I had to teach him to punch from all sorts of angles, to sit down on his shots and turn on them, to unwind his punches in permutations, which he never knew anything about. All he had was a jab and a straight right hand. He had no left hook at all – none whatsoever.

'But we worked day in day out on the same things. It became repetitious. How to turn on his punches, how to pivot on his shots, turn his shoulders. How to get good leverage. And when you have the kind of athletic skills that Lennox has it's not hard to teach. Once it kicks in, then everything else comes so easy.

'His great asset is that he's so tremendously fit. Looking at him, you can tell he's a sportsman, but you don't really know what kind of sportsman he is. I think he could have played any sport he wanted. He could have been a basketball player, a grid-iron footballer. He could have been a tremendous trackman in athletics. It just so happened that boxing was the sport he decided to pursue.

'By the end of the second week you could tell that he was really beginning to learn things. He was picking it up. Everything was falling into place, and I knew then that he had the talent to make it to the top.'

Lennox remembered Davenport from his amateur days. A couple of Montreal boxers – Otis Grant and Howard Grant – spoke to him enthusiastically about John Davenport's boys from New Jersey in the same awed tones as if they were speaking of the Kronk boys from Detroit.

'I knew that John was very dedicated and very regimented,' says Lennox – 'almost like a drill sergeant. But when you're turning professional it's good to have a hard taskmaster. I didn't mind having somebody who was there to push me, always on me.

'I wanted that for myself because in a way I looked on myself as going to war. This was my D-Day, and he was always going to be there like a marine sergeant to remind me to shape up, keep going, and not be soft on myself.'

As for Davenport, he sometimes talks like he's still serving in the marines or doing an impersonation of John Wayne in *Sands of Iwo Jima*. 'I feel a person who lacks discipline is an incomplete person,' he says. 'I feel a person should understand that, and should be able to see where discipline is important. I was trying to make Lennox feel the value of that – the importance of being on time, the importance of sticking to his word, the importance of doing things he is told to do when he is told to do them, more or less by blind faith. Sometimes trying to transform a complete civilian who does not have that discipline is hard.'

For the first fight, at the Royal Albert Hall, Lennox weighed in at 16 st. 7 lb. − 16 lb. heavier than his opponent, Al Malcolm from Birmingham, a journeyman who was Midland-area heavyweight champion.

The six-round bout wasn't top of the bill, but even so Maloney's posters trumpeted the fight as 'The Birth of a Champion'. Lennox, understandably, was anxious to impress. 'I realized that a lot of people would be watching my first fight very critically, and that the whole of my team were depending on me to do well,' he says. 'I was aware that some people were saying that I was all hype, and that I had to prove myself. I was so focused and determined that I can't even remember getting hit. Frank says I took one shot, but I didn't feel it. I walked out in the first round throwing everything. I just wanted to search and destroy.'

The first three minutes were all action, with Lennox looking to knock out Malcolm with every punch he threw. He landed some impressive body punches, and a crashing right hand, before a left hook sent Malcolm down for a count of eight. The Midlander tried to fight back with rights and lefts as Lewis came in with his hands held rather low, but he couldn't beat back Lennox's all-out assault.

Nineteen seconds into the second round, Malcolm threw a looping right hand which missed. In reply Lewis landed a left jab which sent Malcolm front-down on the canvas. There was enough power in the punch to leave him on his knees, squinting with pain, unable to beat the count.

(Frank Bruno, who had been bending down to retrieve his programme, missed the knockout. He said, 'I thought someone had opened the doors at the back of the hall and the draught blew him over.')

The verdict in *Boxing News* was that Lewis had shown power but was over-eager. 'I thought I came through fine,' says Lennox. 'I was never ever worried about losing. I just wanted to win incisively with a bit of style, and I did that.'

The next bit of work experience was to give Lennox a taste of big-fight atmosphere in America. Through his US contact Stan Hoffman, Maloney booked him a fight on the undercard of the Mike Tyson–Carl 'The Truth' Williams heavyweight title fight in Atlantic City, New Jersey, on 21 June 1989.

Again he trained in the Catskills, and the day before the fight the team drove down to New Jersey in an estate van. 'You could feel the excitement in the van because we were going to be part of a title bill,' says Maloney. 'It was our first time in a big American arena, and you could sense an atmosphere of tension amongst us. All except Lennox. I've never seen him get excited about any fight. Whatever happens, this kid is calm and collected. I think he must have ice running through his veins.'

'It was important for me to get used to a professional crowd of that magnitude,' says Lennox. 'If you're not used to that when you come to fight for a title, the excitement and the atmosphere can make you freeze. I blanked the noise of the crowd out. I just wanted to get some experience under my belt and to win, and the fact of fighting in the States was important to me too, because I wanted the American fans to get to know me.'

The fight, at the Convention Hall on the Board Walk, was against Bruce Johnson, of Ohio. The four-rounder was taken purely for experience, for no money and minimal expenses. Johnson was a journeyman who came in the ring 33 lb. lighter than Lewis. Lennox overpowered him for a second-round stoppage (taking only marginally longer than Tyson in the title bout – the referee stopped his fight in the first).

In Britain, Lennox had been installed in a house in Bexley Heath, where he lived with his mother, Violet, and a white poodle called Thai. (Violet wanted to call it Ty, after Mike Tyson, but Lennox told her that that was lacking in respect.)

At first he resisted the idea of living in suburban Kent, but Frank Maloney had insisted. 'I wanted to go back to East London – right back to where I started. But Frank was paranoid to the point that he didn't want me going back to East London. He wanted me to be near him [at that time Frank owned The Crayford Arms in Crayford], so I had no choice in the matter.

'When Frank said he'd got a house for me, I thought, "Great." In Canada most of the houses are detached, and that's the sort of house I had in mind. When he brought me to Kent it was a little town house – all joined up – so I couldn't play my music loud. It seemed so small to me. But I didn't complain – it was just a starting-place. I didn't think I'd be there too long.' (Now Lennox lives in a large house, with a pool-room and a tennis court, in Hadley Wood.)

From 25 September 1989 to 31 January 1990, Lewis had a fight a month. He took February off. Then from March until July he was busy again with a fight a month, and two in May. Mickey Duff – never one to miss the opportunity for a barbed comment where another manager is concerned – accused Maloney of 'doing a Cecil B. De Mille in reverse'. 'They're taking a star and turning him into an unknown,' he said.

The boxing ring was a classroom for Lewis. The big problem for Maloney was finding the right teachers.

The roll call of victims reads as follows:

25 SEPTEMBER 1989, National Sports Centre, Crystal Palace: Andy Gerrard, Risca, Wales. TKO 4 (technical knockout, round four).

10 OCTOBER 1989, City Hall, Hull: Steve Garber, Bradford. KO 1.

5 NOVEMBER 1989, Royal Albert Hall, London: Melvyn Epps, New York. DQ 2. (The American was disqualified for refusing to obey the referee's instructions.)

18 DECEMBER 1989, Kitchener, Ontario: Greg Gorrell, Kansas. TKO 5.

31 JANUARY 1990, York Hall, Bethnal Green: Noel Quarless, Liverpool. TKO 2.

22 MARCH 1990, Leisure Centre, Gateshead: Calvin Jones, Ohio. KO 1.

14 APRIL 1990, Royal Albert Hall, London: Mike Simuwelu, Zambia. KO 1.

9 MAY 1990, Royal Albert Hall, London: Jorge Descola, Argentina. KO 1.

20 MAY 1990, City Hall, Sheffield: Dan Murphy, Nebraska. TKO 6.

27 JUNE 1990, Royal Albert Hall, London: Ossie Ocasio, Puerto Rico. Win on points, eight rounds.

11 JULY 1990, Superstars Nite Club, Mississauga, Ontario: Mike Acey, West Virginia. KO 2.

In eleven fights Lennox had fought for around 90 minutes and had scored ten stoppages. 'I was really very pleased with his progress,' says John Davenport. 'With every fight you could see him growing in confidence and stature. He was on a steep learning-curve, but he's got a very quick mind and picks up lessons very quickly.

'For me the Ocasio fight, where he didn't stop his man. was the best learning fight for Lennox. It was the first time he'd gone the distance. He found out that night that you can't just knock everybody out. And he discovered some important things about himself – that he could pace a fight and had the stamina to go eight rounds. It helped him realize he had the boxing skills to beat a seasoned professional. Ocasio was a very cagey boxer with worlds of experience who won four world-title fights. The fans might not have seen a knockout, but it was a very good learning experience for Lennox.'

'It was like a tutorial for me,' says Lennox. 'Ocasio was very awkward. He wouldn't cooperate in the fight. In fact I wanted to knock him out, but I couldn't knock him out. When we went into the first round he hit me with a right hand, and that shook me up. That's when all of a sudden I switched and I said, "I ain't gonna get hit like that again." That was like a wake-up shot to me, because everything started going slowly and I was brought back to reality.

'It was a good fight for me, because I needed those kind of fights. I would rather have had Ocasio as a sparring partner – he would have taught me a lot – but you can't always get the sparring partners you want.'

Outside the ring, Lennox was getting used to some old English traditions, like dealing with the press and the police. After stopping Andy Gerrard in four rounds, he quipped to reporters, 'It was a very happy fight. I was enjoying hitting him, and he enjoyed getting hit.' A few days later he found himself featured in *The Independent*'s Quotes of the Week.

Another lesson he picked up is that young black people driving a smart car through an expensive white neighbourhood are likely to be stopped by the police.

Three days after his professional debut he was cruising through Bexley Heath in his Mercedes 190E with another black boxer, Antoine Tarver, who had come over from New Jersey for a contest. The company car was one of the perks that went with The Levitt Group deal.

Lennox overtook a car that turned out to be an unmarked police car. Though he wasn't speeding, the police car followed him.

'We were just driving home from Frank's [Maloney's] pub, The Crayford Arms, when we noticed we were being tailed,' he says. 'We didn't think anything of it, because it was an unmarked car. Then all of a sudden loads of cop-cars swooped down on us and told to get out of our car.

'I asked them what was going on. I wasn't used to the police system over here. They wouldn't tell us what was going on. This short cop came over and told me to put my hands on the bonnet, which was hot at the time. He said, "If you move we'll beat you." I told him he was crazy. He was so little there was no way he could touch me. Everyone's little to me. I was insulted that he thought he could beat me.

'Anyway, they took Antoine away, and he's shouting, "What are you doing, man? That's Lennox Lewis." And I'm thinking to myself, "As long as I get one of these cops I'll be satisfied. I'm not going out like Rodney King." But I just keep smiling down at the little guy.

'They still don't tell me anything. They put me in the back of a car, and I was ready to jump out, but there was a nicer guy in the car and he told me, "I think there's a problem with your car."

'At the police station they searched me, but they still didn't tell me what we were being arrested for. They asked me to make a statement, and said did I want it written or tape-recorded. I asked for it to be written, and then made my explanation as long and involved as possible so the cop doing the writing would have a long job. I wanted to be as much a pain to them as they had been to me.

'Then they put me in a cell. I asked them to phone my lawyer, John Hornewer, who had come over to see my first fight. There were some blankets in the cell, so I had a lie-down. By the time John arrived I was sound asleep.

'By this time I was treating it as a joke. I knew I hadn't done anything wrong and that it would be sorted out eventually. It turned out that the car had been repossessed, and the guy who had owned it had reported it stolen. In the end they didn't apologize – they just said it was a big misunderstanding and let us out.

'What was a pest was that two officers kept bugging us for weeks afterwards. They kept coming round wanting us to sign papers to say that we hadn't been mistreated, or whatever, so that we wouldn't sue. It certainly taught me one lesson about England: black guys aren't supposed to drive Mercedes around Bexley Heath.'

There was another odd incident early in his professional career over the fight that wasn't. On 26 February 1990 Lennox was due to box the African champion Proud Kilimanjaro at Crystal Palace. On paper it looked a reasonable fight, though Kilimanjaro's record included some bizarrely named African opponents. He had beaten fighters simply known as Jukebox and Captain Marvel, and somebody called Mary Konate, who, he insisted, was not a woman.

The weigh-in took place, the fight was due to be broadcast live on satellite television, and the crowd were already filing into the seats at the National Sports Centre when the British Boxing Board of Control called the fight off. Lewis was told only twenty minutes before he was due in the ring.

To loud booing from disappointed spectators hoping to see Lennox extend his unbeaten record to eight fights, a joint statement prepared by the Board and Frank Maloney was read from the ring. It said, 'The BBBC have strict medical requirements regarding all boxers coming in to Britain, and medical certificates must be produced. Kilimanjaro and his manager have failed to provide required documents and the Board is not satisfied. Consequently he cannot fight.'

What the rather prim officialese skirted around was the fact that Kilimanjaro had failed to produce a certificate stating that he was not suffering Aids. Since boxing is a sport in which blood can be spilled and exchanged, British boxers are screened every year to make sure they are not HIV-positive. An Aids test is also mandatory for all foreign boxers appearing in this country.

Kilimanjaro – real name Proud Chinembire – took two blood tests at Greenwich Hospital after his arrival in Britain. The first was spoiled when the sample was dropped. A second sample was taken, but the boxer refused to release the test results to anyone but his personal doctor in Harare.

Behind the scenes there had been frantic attempts since four in the afternoon to find a replacement. Last-minute efforts were made to match Lewis with Chris Jacobs, the Welsh champion. First Roger

Levitt wanted to hire a helicopter to fly to collect the boxer, but high winds had closed Swansea and Cardiff airports. When he set off to drive to London, the unfortunate Welshman, who had been offered his biggest pay-day ever (reputedly a five-figure sum), found that the high winds had also closed the Severn Bridge.

Charles Meaden, the then head of Levitt's sports and entertainment subsidiary, recalls, 'Looking back, it was a bit like a stage farce. People were running all over the place on mobile phones trying to find a replacement. When we couldn't find anybody and the crowd had to be told, there was a bit of booing and jeering. Eventually Lennox got up into the ring and quietened them down. It shows what sort of a man he is. Most boxers would have been straight out of the back door and on their way home.'

Lennox says, 'I got up in the ring in my street clothes and said how very disappointed I was. I had trained hard, I was very fit, and I had wanted to knock out Kilimanjaro for them. There was still a bit of argy-bargy after I said that, so I added, "If any of you people booing want to deputize for Kilimanjaro, I'll take on all-comers." '

This had an echo of John L. Sullivan's vaudeville stunt where he used to offer $50 dollars to anyone who could last four rounds with him, issuing the famous boast, 'I can lick any sonofabitch in the house.' At the National Sports Centre, Lennox's challenge was met by a ragged cheer. There were a few punters who claimed they were willing to have a go, but it was only bravado brought on by having spent too long in the bar, and none of them managed to climb into the ring.

13

Death of a Salesman

One of the worst puns ever uttered at a British ringside was made when the ageing Jean-Maurice Chanet entered the ring at the National Sports Centre, Crystal Palace, on Halloween 1990, to defend his European title. 'The Frenchman looks as though he's been around Toulon,' muttered a cynical spectator, 'and he deserves Toulouse.'

Half an hour later the bad joke had proved an accurate forecast, for Lennox Lewis had won his first professional title by pounding the brave but hopelessly outclassed French champion to a six-round defeat.

When Chanet had won the European title earlier in the year, by defeating Commonwealth champion Derek Williams, he became only the fourth Frenchman to do so since compatriot Georges Carpentier became the first title-holder in 1913. Carpentier lost it to the Senegal Frenchman Louis M'barick Fall – a.k.a. 'Battling Siki' – in 1922, then the French had to wait until 1977 for Lucien Rodriguez to lift the title for France again.

Chanet – with a record of twenty-one wins and ten losses – was a surprise winner over Williams in February 1990, and Williams later complained that food poisoning was the reason for his sluggish showing. A rematch was ordered in May, when Chanet beat him again.

But it was always predictable that when Chanet was confronted by the elusiveness and big hitting of Lewis there would be another Agincourt. The thirty-six-year-old gypsy, who ran a candyfloss concession at a fairground near Saint-Dizier, had only turned professional five years earlier. The son of a former fairground wrestler, he had done his training in a circus tent. 'I only box for pleasure,' he said – 'otherwise I would have retired years ago.'

He didn't get much pleasure that Halloween. Lennox used his left jab throughout with great accuracy. He was over a stone heavier than Chanet, with at least a 4-inch height advantage. He prodded the Frenchman's face with the persistence of a pecking gull, and in the first minute the fight was stopped for a doctor to examine a cut in the corner of Chanet's left eye.

Before he entered the ring, it seemed that the Frenchman had been using something akin to old gypsy remedies to secure a victory. In his dressing-room the Boxing Board doctor ordered him to have a full body wash to remove a substance that had been spread over him. He was also relieved of plastic skin, coagulating gels and a linament of doubtful origin. Again before the first bell his cornermen spread grease on the champion's body.

Chanet might have done better attempting to climb into the ring with some lucky white heather and the tattooed lady. The Frenchman showed little skill, if immense courage, and Lewis was able to pick him off at will with a variety of fierce punches. The Swiss referee stepped in to halt the fight after 15 seconds of the sixth round, with Chanet bleeding badly from an ugly cut on the forehead he had sustained in the first.

Chanet returned to the fairground at Saint-Dizier £70,000 richer, and able to fulfil his ambition to purchase his own funfair ride. As for Lennox, Frank Maloney announced that his primary schooling in professional boxing was over. 'It's time to unleash him on the world,' he said.

'Although it was a big fight and the European title was important to me, the Frenchman gave me no trouble,' Lennox says. 'In all those early fights I looked upon it as a street I was travelling down with a goal at the end. I realized there would be curves and bumps on the way, but the goal would always be there. I wanted to win everything that it was possible for me to win – the British, the European, the Commonwealth and then the world title. All those goals were in the master plan – and so was the Canadian title too, but the guy who held that wouldn't fight me.'

Forty-five days earlier Lennox had been one of the guests at a party to celebrate the bar mitzvah of Matthew, one of Roger Levitt's five children. The insurance salesman had a Spanish-style white-stucco fantasy built like a film set in the grounds of his mansion, West Lodge, in Highgate. This was at the apex of the insurance salesman's meteoric rise. That same week the insurance giant Commercial Union had announced that it had paid him £7.35 million for 4.9 per cent of his holding company, The Levitt Group.

The deal valued the company at £150 million, so, at forty-one, Levitt could consider himself worth more than £100 million. Those who worked for him, like Charles Meaden and Frank Maloney in the sports and entertainment division, assumed that the company was as solid as Fort Knox.

As Christmas approached, however, four large investors in the group – Commercial Union, General Accident, Legal & General, and Chase Manhattan – discovered that the company was technically bust. They were told that their previous investments were effectively worthless and were asked to support an emergency £20 million rights issue. They pulled the plug, and on 7 December The Levitt Group was put into administration.

It was a bitter blow for Charles Meaden. Earlier in his career he had been an assistant to the racehorse trainer Barry Hills. He is a man who has been known to have a flutter, but this loss cut him to the bone. 'The whole thing went down on 7 December,' he says. 'The first thing I knew about it was when I was called into this board meeting. I thought we were going in there to get some results for 1990. Levitt just stood up and said, "We are voting for either administration or liquidation."

'It was ridiculous. I'd paid £100,000 just previously for some shares. I owned 2 per cent of a company valued at between £150 million and £200 million. Then nothing. I had to sell the house in the country. It was a disaster. But I'm not the sort of person who puts his head in the sand. My basic talents are contact and people – there's always a role for that. But it just meant that I went from something to nothing within the space of an hour. Now things are fine, but still not the same as they were. It was a big blow.'

The reverberations of the crash were soon felt by the boxing team. Lennox and John Hornewer were actually in the Levitt headquarters that black Friday. 'We were in the offices that night,' says Hornewer. 'We were making phone calls and joking around. We were trying to arrange a fight, but nothing came of it. I forget whose office we were in, but we were sitting there after hours and this notice came round. It said that there would be significant adverse publicity about The Levitt Group. "If you have any questions, contact your supervisor."

'I looked at this thing again and said to Lennox, "You know, something real bad is going to happen." He asked me what I was talking about. I told him I was serious, and said, "If there's anything that you have that you value, get it out of your house and put it somewhere." He said, "Are you serious?" I said, "Yeah, I'm serious – and put the car somewhere else as well." I had an instinct that something was wrong.

'Then that Sunday the article "Death of a Salesman" came out [in the *Mail on Sunday*]. On Monday we actually went into the offices to say goodbye. [Hornewer was returning to Chicago for Christmas, Lennox to Canada.] Roger came out of a meeting to say, "Boys, I need your support." He was pretty gutted, but he was holding up in the circumstances.

'It was traumatic in that we were leading up to the biggest fight so far in Lennox's career – with Gary Mason – and all of a sudden this thing pops.'

For Frank Maloney it was a very worrying period. 'We'd set this thing up. Then, when we'd done all the groundwork and Lennox's promise was beginning to come good, the bottom fell out of it,' he says. 'I tell you, it was a time for steady nerves. It's a good job I had a good team around me and we all pulled together in the same direction.'

The boxing skill of Lennox Lewis was one of the few bankable assets remaining with The Levitt Group that Christmas – a nugget sitting there that the liquidators, KPMG Peat Marwick McLintock, could dispose of. Maloney had to persuade the major creditors – principally Barclays Bank – that, not being in the business of managing boxers, it was in their best interests to get what they could for the contract.

In the early part of 1991 the contract, which runs until 1994, was bought up by Panos Eliades, an accountant who specializes in receiverships, insolvencies and liquidations. Eliades, forty-one, a graduate of Loughborough College and a former self-styled midfield dynamo of Sutton United, says, 'I'd known Lennox for some time, because a neighbour of mine owned his contract.' He laughs and adds, 'My neighbour was called Roger 'The Dodger' Levitt.'

'I went to see a couple of Lennox's fights while he was with Roger, and I got to meet him. There was a rapport between us, and I met him socially a couple of times. Then Roger's company collapsed and they asked me if I was willing to take over the contract, so I stepped in.'

Eliades, whose company PANIX is co-promoter of Lewis's fights, has kept the set-up much as it was, with Frank Maloney still in place as manager and Dennis Lewis as his brother's personal manager.

'You've got to give credit to Frank Maloney for the hard work he put in to put it all back together again,' says John Hornewer. 'We not only had to keep the liquidator situation under control and find other backers, but Frank and I both put up personal money to help finance the training camp for the Mason fight. Though we weren't sure where it was going to end up, we were sure that somebody would want to take over. But we didn't know that we could put the same deal back in place, because a lot of people in the boxing world said Lennox Lewis had bankrupted this guy. That was not the case. I would say the boxing wasn't the least of the Levitt problems, but it wasn't the major problem there.'

Later, Lennox was to give Levitt a job as his commercial manager – a position he held from March 1991 to August 1992. Now he looks back on the period of Levitt's sponsorship of his career with mixed feelings.

'Obviously I'm grateful for what he did for me,' he says. 'He gave me the chance to prove myself. When I walk into a room, I always look into people's eyes, and Levitt was like a motivator. I'd walk in and there seemed to be an aura about him that fascinated me. Every time he spoke, he spoke of millions. He over-emphasized everything. When he would talk of a car it would be the best car, or the best cigars, or how much money he'd made today. He fascinated me, because I actually believed he was doing all those things he was saying. But a lot of it was just talk. He could charm the cream out of coffee.'

His lawyer, John Hornewer, is more harshly critical. 'Having dealt with Roger for three years, nobody can sell me anything any more. I have no time for salespeople, because I've heard the best in the world go at it with me. The first couple of times you meet Roger you buy into it a little bit. But after that you just shut it out. For every word that counts, there are a thousand other words that don't. Basically it's a war of attrition on your patience and your will.'

14

The Only Fear

When Lennox met British champion Gary Mason at Wembley Arena on 6 March 1991, he went into the ring with a brutally simple, cruelly effective strategy: cancel his eyes.

Mason, now an intelligent and wisecracking boxing pundit for Sky TV, was then rated number four in the world. With a 35–0 record and thirty-three knockouts, Mason believed that his edge in experience and power would be too much for Lewis, a comparative novice with only fourteen professional fights behind him.

But the Lewis camp had seen flaws which they aimed to exploit. Mason was a lumbering and pedestrian fighter. He had yet to defeat an active world-ranked contender. Apart from Tyrell Biggs, most of the names on his roster of victims were nonentities. More vitally, he had undergone eye surgery the previous March to repair a detached retina in his right eye.

The plan was simple. In the harsh philosophy of the ring, If you sense a weakness, attack it. Field Marshal Montgomery of Alamein couldn't have got it more wrong when he said, 'There is nothing bellicose about boxing. It is fully in keeping with the principles of the United Nations Organization.'

At training camp, all of Lennox's sparring partners wore white crosses made from tape stuck on the headguards just above the right eye. For seven hard weeks – first in California, then in an old cider barn just outside Bristol – Lennox spent round after round firing his left jab at the white-cross targets. By the time he stepped into the ring to put the plan into operation, he could have found that vulnerable spot on a dark night with his eyes closed.

'When we trained for that fight we chose as our sparring partners men who were exactly the same size as Mason,' says John Davenport. 'We knew he had a bad eye. I know this sounds a bit crude, but I made an X with two strips of tape on the sparring partners' headgear, so Lennox – every day, day in day out – would drill that jab, drill that jab in that eye. If you look at the tape of that fight, that's exactly what he did with Mason. We had that eye sticking out like a baked apple. All the photographs show it.'

Mason – a celebrated trencherman, and one of the few men in the history of British boxing who has emerged from a crash diet at a health farm heavier than when he went in – had gone on another special slimming regime for the fight. This time it worked. At the weigh-in the champion, who sometimes fought at over 17 st., was a relatively svelte 16 st. 11 lb. Before the fight there was some heavy-handed humour along the lines of Lewis giving slimline Mason a fat chance. But, even though the diet had gone well, it couldn't alter the fact that Mason was a statuesque fighter. If he danced at all in the ring, it would be with the nimbleness of a waltzing hippo.

At the pre-fight press conferences, some genuine needle crept in. Mason threatened all sorts of painful mayhem – almost suggesting that it was beneath his dignity to be confronted by such a novice.

'Gary is in a glasshouse throwing stones,' said Lennox. 'He deals in hype; I deal in reality.

'He doesn't know how strong I am, how determined. He has no idea of the strategy I will adopt from the first bell.'

'I really mean business,' replied Mason. 'I said he wouldn't turn up, and I don't believe he wants this fight. He's a victim of circumstances, and that worry is in his mind.'

Lennox turned up all right, and implemented his plan of attack from the start. His left jab shot through Mason's palsied defence and sent a spray of sweat off his unprotected head. Lewis sometimes used his right with economy and effect, but it was the left jab – thumping home like a tactical missile – that did most of the damage. Lewis might have finished it earlier, but Mason's courage, and a heart as big as Jamaica, kept him going until the seventh, when he was forced to retire from the fight – and from boxing. At the end it looked as though his face had been in collision with a steamroller, and later he had to have more surgery on his eye.

'At the end of the fifth and sixth I was scolding Lennox in his corner,' says Davenport. 'I said, "Look, we have come too far, we have worked too hard. Why are you carrying this man? We've got him drunk as a skunk. We've got him ready to go. Let's get out of here." So we finished it, and I felt really good.'

So far the newspapers had been grudging in their praise of Lewis, scornful that his first dozen fights hadn't been a real examination of his ability – mere GCSEs when he should have been sitting the first part of his tripos. But now the *Daily Express* trumpeted his win with the headline 'At last a Brit Heavy's looking the part.' Their man at the ringside, James Lawton, wrote:

Lennox Lewis will never be Frank Bruno. He will never invade our hearts. But then maybe nor will he insult our intelligence.

We should learn to love him anyway for one great shining possibility. The new British champion with the soft Canadian accent . . . might just step into a world title ring with more purpose than the collection of a huge blood-smeared cheque . . . Lewis has more potential than any British heavyweight since the war.

'The British title was important to me,' says Lennox, 'but what motivated me too was the fact that I didn't want to lose to Mason. I thought he had dissed me [disrespected me] by saying that I wasn't really good enough to get in the ring with him. It was a battle of the egos – his and mine.

'In the fight, I wasn't particularly going for his eyes – I was going after his face. If you hit a guy enough times in the face, especially with my jab – it's a sharp and piercing jab anyway – it will bust it up. So it wasn't just his eye all banged up and swollen – it was his whole face.'

A few days later Lennox was involved in another battle of the egos when he met Olympic gold-medallist and world-champion sprinter Linford Christie for a TV stunt. ITV commentator Jim Rosenthal asked Lennox whether he thought the runner would make a good boxer. Lennox smiled and told him, 'No. He looks more like a lover than a fighter – a sweet boy.'

Christie, not put off by the slight, then said that he was prepared to step in the ring with Lewis for a £2 million purse. 'I've got it all worked out,' he said. 'I hit you and then run – and you've got to catch me.'

That March, with a nimbleness that Christie would have envied, Roger Levitt found himself back in the boxer's corner. This time the roles were reversed. The silver-tongued businessman wasn't funding the Lennox Lewis operation any more – he was one of its paid employees. Four months after the collapse of The Levitt Group, the bankrupt financial adviser became Lewis's commercial manager. 'It feels like I'm coming out of a bad dream,' he said.

His job was to line up sponsorship deals for the heavyweight. 'He could make up to £20 million in sponsorship in the next two years,' he claimed. 'As world champion, in 1992 his boxing earnings could be £50 million.'

Levitt was pleased that he would be on a percentage. 'The money in boxing is enormous. There is no other business where I can make this sort of money. My creditors are delighted.'

He had, he said, been offered seven figures to write a book about himself and to make a film, but, at just forty-one, he thought it was a bit soon – though he didn't rule it out. 'Once Lennox Lewis is world champion perhaps I will.'

'Lennox considered me to be the best salesman he'd ever met,' he says. 'Obviously he'd seen what I'd built. And, whilst I lost all that, at least I had it once – which I guess is a lot more than most people. I could look back with a little pride, as obviously Lennox had done. Then he felt that if he could assist me to assist him further, that was a winning combination.'

Levitt was back again in a prominent position in the boxer's entourage. He enjoyed the glitz of big fights, basking in the warm glow radiating from the fighter's growing reputation. At times he acted as though the crash of the previous December had never happened and he was still the power behind the whole operation.

Lennox Lewis is a calm and patient man, but eventually Levitt's attitude was to light the slow-burning fuse of Lennox Lewis's anger.

The only British-born boxer to hold the world heavyweight title before Lennox Lewis picked up his WBC belt was Bob Fitzsimmons.

Robert Prometheus Fitzsimmons – 'Ruby Bob' – was a spindle-legged, freckly man, with carroty receding hair – the ugliest and most unlikely looking heavyweight champion in the history of the sport. He was just under 6 feet, knock-kneed and gangling. Below his waist he was built like a wading-bird. As the boxing historian O. F. Snelling wrote, 'Stripped for action he looked like an elderly red pelican.' But he had a huge, sinewy upper body, with strong arm and back muscles developed when he had toiled as an apprentice blacksmith.

Although he was a natural middleweight, he was such a skilled fighter (he invented the punch to the solar plexus) that he fought some of the best big men at the turn of the century.

He was born in Helston, Cornwall, on 4 June 1862, but his family emigrated to New Zealand when he was a child of nine and he never returned to England. Bob learned his boxing in New Zealand and Australia, where the great bare-knuckle fighter Jem Mace ran a pub in Sydney with a boxing saloon attached to it. He died a US citizen in Chicago in 1917 at the age of fifty-five.

He was the first man in the history of boxing to win three world championships in three separate weight divisions. He won his heavy-weight title – the one whose glory we've eked out all this century – at Carson City, Nevada, on St Patrick's Day 1897, when he knocked out 'Gentleman Jim' Corbett.

It was near Carson City that Lennox trained for his next fight. It was to be held in an outdoor arena on the site of an old volcano 6,300 feet up in the Sierra Nevada at Lake Tahoe.

'Being there in the place that meant so much to British boxing was a strange feeling,' says Lennox. 'All the people in our training camp made a little pilgrimage around the place to try to imagine what it had been like ninety-four years earlier when Fitzsimmons won the title.

'It got me to thinking about how people had been saying in the papers that I wasn't really British – like I was some sort of mercenary who'd come over here from Canada purely for the money. But Fitzsimmons left England when he was nine – and some books say he was only six. Already when my mum sent for me to join her in Canada I'd lived in Britain for twelve years – 25 per cent longer than he ever did. But I figured that if I did win the heavyweight title there would be no question about it – straight away the British would claim me as a natural-born son.'

In *The Times* in January 1993, Simon Barnes wrote, 'One of the greatest examples of the blurring of boundaries is the boxer Lennox Lewis: he is British, Canadian, and Jamaican all at once: a citizen of the world: a time traveller from the next century.'

'That summed it up very well for me,' says Lennox. 'Simon put into words something I'd felt for a long time. There are bits in me from all three cultures. Part of me is British, and no one can deny that. I was born here and I'm a West Ham supporter – how much more British can I get?

'But there is part of me that's Jamaican too. Both of my parents come from there. I'm black. Since I've been going back there, I've got very close to the island, its people, its culture and its music. And its weather too. I like it there.

'But, in the same way, there's a bit of me that's Canadian as well. I went to school there. I learned my boxing there, I grew to manhood there, I won a gold medal for Canada at the Olympics, so a cherished part of me must still belong to Canada.

'How I look at it is this way: I'm a world champion, and I want to be a champion of the whole world. I want to belong to everybody. Just like Barnes said, I want to be a citizen of the world. As for the last bit, I don't think I'm ready to become a time traveller from the next century yet. I'm still working on that one.'

In the rarefied air of the Sierra Nevada, Lennox made a big impression on his opponent, Mike Weaver, and on Americans who were watching him for the first time on television. Because of Weaver's retreating style it was an awkward fight for Lewis, and there was some desultory booing when the crowd became restive at his inability to provide a quick knockout punch. But when it came it arrived with goodbye-time accuracy.

Mike Weaver, who, at forty, still looked like a sculpted Hercules, was a grandfather. It was a fact that provoked a few derisive comments. The *Sun* headlined the fight, 'Lewis to beat up a grandad.' Although Weaver's best days were behind him, he remained a cagey veteran who would give Lennox a boxing tutorial. Lured out of retirement by the success of that other pugilistic senior citizen George Foreman, he was a boxer of impressive experience. He had had seven world-title fights, had held the WBA title in 1980, and had boxed a career total of 337 rounds.

Lennox was odds-on favourite to win, but he couldn't take chances. Lewis had to fight six patient rounds before he could get in his telling right-hander. Before that he picked up a cut over his right eye – the first time he'd been cut in a pro fight – as the result of a clash of heads.

Several times the foxy Weaver retreated to the ropes, hoping to lure Lewis after him. Lennox refused to take the bait and backed away, drawing jeers.

'I'd seen so many tapes of Weaver that I knew exactly what he was trying to do. I'd seen him knock out Carl "The Truth" Williams after bringing him on to the ropes so he could nail him. I wasn't going to fall for it,' says Lennox.

Trainer John Davenport insists that Lennox fought a disciplined fight, boxing perfectly to orders. 'In the tapes, when Williams hurt Weaver in the middle of the ring, Weaver automatically went back to the ropes. Carl followed him, and Weaver threw that left hook that knocked Carl out. I said to Lennox, "Look, we do not want to be suckered in. You can always tell when you hurt a man and he's going back on the ropes because you drive him there, but you can also tell when a man is going back to try to sucker you into a trap."

'In round two Lennox hurt him with a right hand. And what did Weaver do? He retreated straight to the ropes. Lennox started after him and he remembered. He remembered what we had studied on the tapes, and he backed off.

'Now the media, right away, jumped on him. They said that Lennox should have finished him right then. But they didn't know what our game plan was. Lennox ended up stopping Weaver four rounds later in the middle of the ring. Weaver threw out a slow jab, and Lennox countered with a fast right hand over the top and knocked him stiff. And I was proud of him, because he went totally by what we had studied and planned to do.'

Another electrified spectator was Emanuel Steward of the Kronk Gym, Detroit. 'I was very, very impressed by what I saw,' he said. 'I think he's a future world champion. He handled Weaver very well, and Weaver is someone I wouldn't put any of my fighters in with.

'Realistically, Lewis is probably six or seven fights away from the world title. But I would put him in with Tyson tomorrow, because I think he would beat him.'

Saturday 21 September 1991 is the day British boxing had to examine its conscience and take stock of itself. In the twelfth round, at the end of a fiercely contested middleweight title fight, brave but exhausted Michael Watson collapsed from an upper-cut delivered by the champion, Chris Eubank.

The punch sent Watson to the edge of death. A blood clot had to be removed from his brain. He spent months in hospital, deep in coma, blacked out by traumatic head injuries. Even now, after two years of therapy for brain injuries resulting in slurred speech and partial paralysis, Michael is still struggling to regain a shadow of his once sublime fitness.

His devastating injuries, whose impact was made worse by the image of the victor giving an insensitive interview on live TV as his opponent lay stricken on the ring apron, led to a period of intense self-examination within the boxing community. The very existence of the sport came under the microscope of public debate as people confronted the dangerous consequences which darken boxing, and the crass hard sell and phony grudge elements that, increasingly, were being built into big fights.

The discussion was even more pointed because, as Watson lay in his drugged and deathly sleep, wired to a life-support system, nine days later Lennox Lewis was due to meet Glenn McCrory in a televised fight for the British and European heavyweight titles.

During the last week of the build-up to the McCrory fight, Lennox's handlers were accused of insensitivity for throwing down a £2 million challenge to Frank Bruno while boxing was trying to come to terms with the tragedy of Michael Watson.

Gary Mason, whose British title Lennox had recently won, complained, 'People like that have just no sense – they must be stupid. The last thing you want to be talking about at this moment is another big fight. We should just be praying for Michael. It's sickening. You know the show has to go on, but there are certain things you do and don't do at a time like this to give ammunition to the anti-boxing lobby.'

Frank Maloney was quick to insist that the offer was not ill-timed. 'We feel desperately concerned about Michael Watson,' he said, 'but we are in a business and we are all boxing people. If we had cancelled today's conference, we would have been admitting that boxing has a problem. No one holds a gun to a boxer's head about fighting.' (The offer to Bruno came to nothing. He was making a comeback after eye surgery, and chose easier opponents than Lewis.)

Lennox admitted that he had been shaken by what he had seen on television the previous Saturday, but he still intended to fight – and to beat McCrory. 'I am in a deep state just thinking about it [Watson's injury],' he said. 'I feel that the whole country should be praying for his recovery and his family.

'I've taken a little time out to pray for Michael. But we've got to put recent events out of our minds. I've got to be 100 per cent focused going into the ring. This is the job we have taken on – every boxer knows the danger that could lie ahead.'

At the Royal Albert Hall on the night of the fight, there were reminders of the previous week's tragedy. Jimmy Tibbs, one of McCrory's cornermen, was Watson's trainer. Paramedics with stretchers were in obvious evidence. The British Boxing Board of Control had decreed that ITV should not conduct its post-fight interview in the ring, where emotions run high, but in a dressing-room, where interviewers and boxers are more composed.

Glenn McCrory, a former IBF cruiserweight champion, who had sparred ninety-six rounds with Mike Tyson and emerged to tell the tale, had spent time training with the Green Howards Regiment at Catterick. Though he was only 10 lb. lighter than Lewis, when he entered the ring behind the pipes and drums of the Green Howards he looked what he was – no more than a blown-up cruiserweight.

The soldiers could offer him little help when the bout began. It only took Lewis 270 seconds to take McCrory apart and retain his British and European titles. His reach was 3 inches longer than McCrory's, and he seemed to be able to land punches at will.

Lennox concentrated on the body – the area which the American Jeff Lampkin had exploited to take away McCrory's cruiserweight title. Then he switched to the head, and the challenger was lucky to make it to the sanctuary of the bell that ended round one.

A short right hand put McCrory to his knees at the start of round two. The referee, John Coyle, had reached nine before the boxer righted himself. McCrory mounted a brief flurry, but then another big right-hander put him down on all fours and he was counted out as he tried to haul himself off the canvas.

It was quick and, mercifully, McCrory suffered no permanent damage apart from a busted nose. In defeat he was generous: 'Mike Tyson never manhandled me like that,' he admitted. 'Lewis is very much up there with him and Evander Holyfield. He is so fast. I've been in with a number of world-class fighters, and no one has done that to me.'

Looking back, Lennox says, 'It was a difficult week. There was a lot of concern and genuine emotion about Michael's condition, and of course something like that has to be at the back of your mind as you build up to a contest. But as soon as the bell goes you have to put it out of your mind.

'Boxers are very focused men. You mustn't let your mind wander on to anything else when you're boxing. If you're not concentrating 100 per cent then you're courting disaster. There's a man across the ring who's trying to take the top of your head off – you've always got to be aware of that.

'I play a lot of chess, and you've got to think a fight through as carefully as a chess match. You're using all your best strategies and tactics against this man, whatever he is coming at you with. You spend weeks and weeks of preparation working on schemes and tactics, getting ready to counter his attacks and surprise him with some of your own.

'People tend to forget that boxers are professionals. We don't just turn up and put the gloves on – this is our job; this is what we do. We're highly trained. People ask boxers whether they're frightened of getting into the ring. It's like asking the pilot of Concorde if he's frightened of taking off. If you're doing a job you're trained for, fear doesn't come into it.

'The only fear I have is the fear of losing. I don't feel fear of pain, or fear of my opponent, because I have prepared myself to deal with anything that happens in a fight. Defeat is a humiliation, and you fear that. The beaten boxer always loses some of his manhood. Defeat is undignified. The loser is either flat on his back or bowed down and exhausted in his corner. That's what every boxer trains so hard to avoid.

'There is always a possibility that any man going into a ring could get as badly hurt as Michael Watson. But boxers are athletes, and all athletes take risks. Accidents are fickle things. I could hurt myself walking across my lawn, or playing tennis in my back garden.

'Boxing is the life I've chosen and the risk I've decided to take. People climb Everest and then suddenly five of them fall off the mountain and die. And people are asking, "Why, why, why?" Well, just because – because we're human beings, and we test ourselves with challenges.'

Violet, Lennox's mother, was a spectator at the Watson fight. Being there affected her deeply. 'It was so sad for Michael and his family. It's really hard whenever something so rough and undeserved happens to such nice people,' she says.

'I go to all of Lennox's fights, and I sit there all the time praying – praying that nothing happens to Lennox and nothing happens to the boy he's fighting. I'm not biased in my prayers – I just hope that God looks after both of them. I don't want Lennox ever to get really hurt, and if he did I'd be the first one to tell him to pack it in. No amount of money is worth giving up your health for, and he's got a whole life ahead of him to enjoy yet.

'A few years ago there was a mother who got up in the ring and started hitting the guy who was beating her boy. She took off her shoe and started hitting him over the head with it. Everybody made a big joke of it and said she was a typical woman, but she was only doing what a lot of mothers would feel like doing. She was a typical mother, that's all.

'If ever I thought that Lennox was in bad trouble in the ring, I'd stop it. I wouldn't care what people thought of me, I'd climb up there and stop it somehow. I'd never want Lennox to be hurt as badly as poor Michael Watson was.'

15

Exit

The Horizontal Heavyweight

Lewis had an unblemished 17–0 record. His career was on course. In the space of twenty-six months he had won and defended the British and European titles. Good judges of boxing ability had predicted that soon he would win a world title. Yet all was not euphoric in the boxer's camp.

The acerbic character of trainer John Davenport grated on manager Frank Maloney. His training methods had provoked murmurs of dissent in the gym. Even more damaging to his future involvement was the fact that Lennox himself had begun to doubt the benefits of his coaching.

Davenport was not particularly happy having to live for long periods exiled from America at an obscure address in Upper Belvedere, Kent. He missed home. Worse still he missed his two children – Michael, then nine, and daughter Ebony, nineteen. He was a lonely, sensitive man, whose devotion to boxing had cost him his marriage. He still ordered his life as though it was run by service regulations. He belonged to that army tradition which believed that you could tell someone to move something from A to B without telling him why. It was as though, metaphorically, he was still wearing his old marine sergeant's uniform, with two chips on each shoulder. Visitors to his gym were, as like as not, regarded like a platoon of visiting Vietcong.

'We were giving him a good living out of boxing – one that he'd never had before. He had a home and a car, yet all he did all the time was moan,' says Maloney. 'It just wasn't good enough for him. I can't count the arguments I had with him.

'At one meeting I made a point of telling him that trainers and managers were only as good as the boxers they handled. The trainer and the manage aren't the stars: the boxer is. It wasn't as though he had a complete novice to handle – in Lennox he had someone with a winner's pedigree. All he had to do was iron out some of his amateur habits and bring him on. It wasn't a case of back to the drawing-board, let's start again. All of Lennox's marvellous talent was already there.

'I think John is a great amateur trainer. Bring him a boy of seven or eight and you could guarantee that by the time he was twenty the boy would be a good fighter. But I don't think the way he operated worked with the mature twenty-six-year-old boxer we had.'

On 23 November 1991, at the Omni Arena, Atlanta, Georgia, Lennox was to meet Tyrell Biggs, on the undercard of the Evander Holyfield–Bert Cooper heavyweight title fight. Biggs was the boxer who had beaten him in the quarter-finals of the Los Angeles Olympics in 1984. Since winning the gold medal there, Biggs's professional career – which initially promised so much – had proved a disappointment.

In seven years he had gone from title-contender to fodder for ranked and rising fighters. Biggs had the kind of hit-and-run style suited to the amateur ranks but often exposed in the crash-bang-wallop frenzy of the professional game. He torpedoed his prospects when he succumbed to a cocaine habit at the start of his pro career, and he never looked quite the same after his rehabilitation from drugs.

His blighted promise was a justification for the softly-softly approach Frank Maloney had taken with Lewis. Biggs had fought some difficult slugging fights without enough seasoning to get himself accustomed to the change of style. He had suffered as a result. In a fight against David Bey in March 1987 he stopped Bey in the sixth round, but only after his opponent had opened up a cut over Biggs's left eye that needed thirty-two stitches to repair.

In a heavyweight title fight on 19 October the same year, Mike Tyson had knocked him out in seven rounds. Tyson said he knew he had him in the third, because Biggs was making noises when he hit him in the body. Asked what type of noises, Tyson replied, 'Like a woman screaming.'

Lennox had improved immeasurably since his last meeting with Biggs. Then he was a nervous eighteen-year-old over-awed by fighting the home-boy in the fiercely partisan atmosphere of the Los Angeles games. Now he was mature in strength and mind, and it took him only three rounds to finish Biggs.

Lewis had the look of a future champion as he dispassionately zeroed in on his opponent. He leapt from his stool at the opening bell and dominated from the start. As usual, the best left-jabber in heavy-weight boxing relied on his stinging jabs to open the way for the hard right crosses that followed. He went through his repertoire of moves and combinations, throwing in the occasional straight right and jolting Biggs's head back with upper-cuts when he moved in to clinch.

In the third, a chopping Lennox right had Biggs spinning to the canvas for the first knockdown. Biggs was on his feet at eight, but down again when Lewis pounced with another right cross. He beat the count, but a third right put him down for the last time. Florida referee Frank Santore, under the three-knockdown rule, signalled the end of the proceedings.

'In the Olympics I could never quite catch up with him. He was very elusive,' says Lewis. 'But in Atlanta I cut off his escape routes, and he couldn't get away from me. I always knew I had the beating of him. I was primed to win the return – I had been waiting seven years to pay him back.'

The clinical efficiency of Lennox's victory impressed one highly influential spectator – Seth Abraham, president of Time–Warner

Sports, which owns the HBO TV network, was delighted with the way Lewis had gone about his job. 'Lennox was seen coast to coast across the United States. I estimate there were at least 25 million people watching him, and I'm sure most of them were as impressed as I was. That was the night I became convinced that Lennox was going to erase that old cliché about the horizontal British heavyweight for good.'

It was a time of turmoil in the heavyweight division. Mike Tyson had been accused of rape by Desiree Washington and was awaiting trial. His removal from the scene meant that Don King had no direct involvement in sport's richest prize, and that left the way open for other promoters and managers to wheel and deal.

The incumbent, Evander Holyfield, controlled by the Duvas, had shown against Bert Cooper that he would struggle against a genuine heavyweight who was talented. Only the superb conditioning of the smaller, lighter Holyfield got him through against Cooper to win by a technical knockout in the seventh. Now big men with big punches – Riddick Bowe, Razor Ruddock and Lennox – began to fancy their chances against Holyfield and moved in on the champion like circling birds of prey.

'The heavyweight title is up for grabs,' said Lennox, 'I want to get to Holyfield first.' Unfortunately for British hopes of an undisputed heavyweight title, Riddick Bowe beat him to it. Frank Maloney suspected that he would all along. 'I sincerely believed that Lennox was the only contender with real credibility. Unfortunately the Americans were scared that he would take the heavyweight title away from them. There was a lot of politics involved, and in some ways Lennox was too good for his own good. He scared them all off.'

After the cool efficiency of his demolition of Biggs, Lennox's next fight, on 1 February 1992, was a disappointment. He made his Las Vegas debut and was taken ten rounds for the first time in his career. The match against Levi Billups, a thirty-one-year-old former line-backer and wrestler, was an awkward one for Lewis. There had been a late switch of opponents, and Lewis learned he was going to fight Billups on the 'Night of the Young Heavyweights' bill only a week before the contest. Lennox blames it on politics: 'The guys we wanted to fight, HBO said were no good. Yet they allowed Riddick Bowe to fight those kind of guys all the time. It was a whole heap of politics. I don't know whether it was because I was from Britain and he was American, or they were trying to build Bowe up as a celebrity, but it was a problem for us.'

Billups was built like a dumper-truck, and Lennox found it difficult to put him away. From the early rounds Billups showed that his first instinct was to survive, but he still managed to sting Lewis with fierce upper-cuts in the third and final rounds.

The judges gave the result to Lennox 10–0, 9–1 and 8–2. But Lewis had learned some hard lessons: how to contend with a tough, flailing, awkward opponent, and how to pace himself over ten strenuous rounds.

The fight was the last one for trainer John Davenport, who, understandably, is still bitter about his exit from the team. 'I am deeply hurt,' he says.

'There were some things I did not like about Lennox. He was not the kind of person I was used to being associated with as far as sticking by his people is concerned. What I mean by that is that he did not always live by his word – and that is not to put him down. I am trying to be as nice about him as I possibly can be. It's just that I am a street person, OK? When someone's with you, they're supposed to be with you all the way.

'I was trying to make him a complete fighter. And if you look at the tapes of Lennox from his very first professional fight, then view one of the middle ones, and then one towards the end when I was with him, you would see that transformation – you would see a complete fighter. He was a guy who was 6 feet 5 inches who could box equally well inside as he could box outside. That is a rarity. Most tall men cannot box at all inside. Muhammad Ali was one. As good as he was, he could not box at all inside.'

Davenport thinks his assertiveness got him the sack. 'I am too outspoken. That's a problem that a lot of people have had with me in the past,' he says. 'If I see something that's not right, I can't just shut my eyes to it. To some people, the way they looked at it, I was always creating a disturbance. If something's not right, I speak up – I don't go to the back door with someone.

'The thing is, I had been taught that the coach is the boss, and you have to do what he says. The problem is that boxers earn so much money that when they have got a bit in the bank they think they know it all. That's one of the problems. They are their own worst enemies. They have no loyalty. They cannot spell the word "loyalty". That is the sad part about boxing – they do not understand loyalty.'

Lennox refuses to get into a slanging match. 'I understand why John feels like that – I just came to the conclusion that his training methods were making me too robotic. He was taking me away from my natural style, trying to restrict me to set patterns and make me box by numbers. My great strengths are mobility, speed and the ability to surprise. I felt he curbed my freedom to express myself. God gave me a lot of talents, and I realized I wasn't using them all.

'He made me feel that everything I was doing was wrong, and that attitude of his affected the whole team. Under him, nobody was particularly happy in the gym.

'To me, in a sense, John Davenport wasn't happy unless he was miserable, and it was spoiling the overall aura of the team and my progression. I spoke to him plainly and said I didn't think it was right any more. He asked me to reconsider. I said I had reconsidered, and it was no easy decision for me to make.'

The man they brought in as the new trainer was Pepe Correa, fifty-two, a Puerto Rican who grew up in New York. Previously he had been amateur trainer to Sugar Ray Leonard, starting with him when Leonard was fourteen. Ray Charles Leonard – one of the most stylish and skilful boxers of the age – was welterweight champion at the Montreal Olympics and went on to win world titles at five weights. Correa rejoined Leonard as professional trainer at the end of his career, when his record under Pepe was 2 fights, 1 won, 1 lost.

Correa – whose other charges have inclucded Dan Sherry and Andrew Maynard – is a sharp dresser, with a taste of souped-up cars. He calls Lennox 'Big Guy'. 'Lennox is a massive individual, but what really strikes you about him is his ability to move,' he says. 'You would expect that he would be stationary, but he's not at all.

'I saw that ability to move in the 1988 Olympics, but subsequently it was taken away from him. I think that's why I was brought in – to bring that movement back. Not every trainer works with every boxer. You've got trainers who are good with sluggers, or good with boxers, or with guys that are plodders. That's not to take it away from the previous trainer – it's just that he was trying to teach the wrong man the wrong thing. He was taking away his mobility, and when you take away this young man's mobility you take away the best of the fighter.'

The testy former sergeant doesn't mince words in his opinion of Correa. He says he's a bad trainer but 'a great motivator – what we call in America a cheer-leader. But if a fighter gets hurt and comes back to the corner you have to tell him to go from A to Z, and you have to be able to tell him how to get there. That is one of the things Pepe Correa cannot do. That's not disrespect – that's just plain fact.'

Oddly enough, Correa was impressed by Lennox's performance in the Billups fight – the contest before Davenport's dismissal. 'You know what brought me to the conclusion that Lennox could go all the way? It was when I watched the Levi Billups fight on TV. Billups is the kind of guy who can make you look very bad when you fight him, because he's so awkward. He's strong, he's compact, he's hard to hit clean. When you do hit him, he's got a very good chin. To be able to stay there, go the distance with him, yet win convincingly, showed me that Lennox had something.'

Correa took charge of the training programme for Lewis's next fight. It was a triple-title showdown at the Royal Albert Hall on 30 April 1992. Lennox put his British and European titles on the line, hoping to wrest the Commonwealth title from the Londoner Derek 'Sweet D' Williams.

Lennox took only 8½ minutes to stop Williams, but he looked over-eager in the first two rounds, and the failure of his attempts to blast Williams away had the crowd chanting 'Bruno, Bruno' at him at the end. Lennox told them, 'I hear you chanting for Bruno. If you want Bruno to fight me, you bring him on.'

It had all come good in round three. Pepe Correa told him in the corner, 'Forget what we did in the gym – just go out and knock him out.' Reckless advice maybe, but Lennox did just that – finishing off Williams with a perfect right-left-right combination. The first short right detonated on Sweet D's chin, quickly followed by the other two. He went crashing to the canvas in the red corner, his 16 st. 9 lb. hitting the ring floor with the noise of a side of beef being thrown off a lorry.

Referee Larry O'Connell got to the count of nine, then Williams, who had never been stopped before in twenty-two fights, managed to get to his feet. But he stood against the ropes with his arms dangling by his sides, obviously not wanting to take any further part in the action.

'Williams is a nice, friendly guy and I like him,' says Lennox, 'but you can't let things like that interfere with your work. He did make things look awkward for me for a couple of rounds, but I knew I would get him in the end. He was talking to me, saying, "You can punch harder than that." Then I suckered him into my upper-cut.'

Correa was pleased with his first night's work. 'What makes Lennox a great fighter is that he's so relaxed, so assured of himself,' he says. 'You see it in every fight. I saw it that night against Williams. When he walks into the ring on fight nights, pay attention to him. You can see it in his eyes: "I know I can beat you." It's not the silly game of out-staring or out-facing the other man that some boxers go in for. Lennox is very quiet, but he's oh so confident – the other guy sees it straight away. Lennox has this calm but solid conviction in his ability. He knows that once the other guy gets in the ring he's a beaten man.'

That summer the deal was put in place to resolve the pecking order in the heavyweight division. The champion, Evander Holyfield, who between 1986 and 1988 had successfully defended the world cruiserweight title five times, still looked unconvincing in the top weight division.

In Tokyo on 11 February 1990, James 'Buster' Douglas had surprised the whole world, himself and – most of all – Don King by knocking out Mike Tyson in the tenth round of their title fight. Then, having spent years as a contender who pre-Tyson had never taken his big chances, he decided to taste the good life – in a very big way. In the next eight months he went on an eating binge, swallowing his favourite meals with the efficiency of a demented cement-mixer. When he climbed back into the ring on 25 October he looked like a junk-food mountain, and few were surprised when Holyfield knocked him out in three rounds. (Defeat didn't stop the eating. In retirement Buster looks, according to *Sports Illustrated*, 'like a helium balloon after the gas has been left on too long'. At thirty-three he weighs a very snug 22 st. 12 lb.)

Hard as he trained, Holyfield never looked a convincing heavyweight. He laboured against Bert Cooper. Though he beat those feisty representatives of Grandad's Army, George Foreman and Larry Holmes, both veterans took him the full twelve rounds.

After he had beaten Holmes on 19 June 1992, Holyfield's team of Dan and Lou Duva set up with Frank Maloney and the other interested parties the deal that promised to give Lennox his title shot. He would meet Donovan 'Razor' Ruddock in London on 31 October, and the winner of that fight would take on the victor of the Evander Holyfield–Riddick Bowe title match which would take place at Las Vegas on 13 November. Before Ruddock, Lennox would have a warm-up fight on 11 August 1992 against Mike Dixon at Hurrah's Casino, Atlantic City.

The ringside at the Casino was like a *Who's Who* of heavyweight contenders. The spectators included Bowe and his manager Rock Newman, and Ruddock and his coach, the former champion Floyd Patterson.

Lennox arrived from his Maryland training camp aware that he was under scrutiny. But it didn't faze him. 'They won't know what to expect even by seeing the Dixon fight. I am a boxer who boxes according to what the opponent puts before me.'

This particular opponent didn't put much. Dixon was 26 lb lighter than Lennox, who did as he pleased for three rounds before becoming the first man to stop Dixon, in the fourth.

Lennox began the fight with six stinging and unanswered left jabs, and then followed with a right cross. Still operating behind the left jab, he started unloading thumping rights to the body. Dixon's only response was a left hook on the bell. Lennox cruised in the second, but put together one four-punch combination that hit Dixon like the back of a shovel. Dixon grinned – a sure sign he had been hurt.

In the third and fourth, Lennox abandoned all caution and piled in booming right hands. He began the fourth with five successive rights and a left to the body. Dixon wilted under the attack, and referee Rudy Battle gave him a standing count of eight. Lewis moved in again with two big rights, and, as Dixon blundered around the ring like a stunned heifer, Battle ended it after 62 seconds of the fourth.

Bowe and Ruddock were predictably scornful. 'Who was he fighting anyway?' Bowe asked, 'He shouldn't have let that guy go four rounds. Lewis should have knocked him cold.' Ruddock joined the chorus and said, 'He won't be able to take the pressure and my most important objective on the night will be to knock him out. I have the same confidence as when I arrived, but I am not going to underestimate Lewis.'

Lennox, who was hardly sweating at the end of four rounds, saw it differently. He said, 'I showed Razor I'm not going to be easy to fight, and I know he was feeling some of those right hands that I gave Dixon. I hope he learned a couple of things.

'I felt good. I was relaxed, and I just went out and was boxing – doing what comes naturally. I was not surprised I didn't knock him over – he was just in defensive mode. I wanted to give him a boxing lesson, but he got a bit feisty and wanted to hit me so I had to take him out.'

Floyd Patterson, who had won his heavyweight title thirty years earlier, is a civilized man who has no need to bad-mouth anybody. He offered a more generous assessment of Lewis. 'He keeps calm and he's very confident and smooth,' he said. 'He's a devastating puncher, and he can take opponents out with one punch. There's going to be two big-hitters in that London ring.'

There was an even bigger showdown happening outside the ring at Atlantic City. Hurrah's Casino was the setting for Levitt's Last Hurrah. Lewis had become increasingly irritated by Roger Levitt's showy overstatement at his big fights. He was merely Lennox's commercial manager, but he behaved like the great panjandrum – implying with a nudge, a wink and a say-no-more that he was still the power behind it all.

'I felt that if Roger had focused his attention solely on getting endorsements for Lennox he might be able to help,' says John Hornewer, the attorney. 'But Roger started trying to involve himself in the boxing more and more – contacting HBO, trying to establish a personal relationship with Seth Abraham at Time–Warner Sports, telling people that he was still the man behind Lennox Lewis. And he was undermining Frank Maloney.

'Lennox is the kind of person who will give you rope. You can either make the rope into something pretty or you can hang yourself with it. He has a long fuse in these things. But Roger's time was up – he had exhausted his welcome. The final straw was at the Mike Dixon fight at Atlantic City. Basically Roger was told not to come. But he came, and Lennox reacted. That was the time that Roger made his announcement that he was resigning his position due to personal obligations and family illness. You can read into that whatever you want.'

At the time, Roger Levitt's mother was gravely ill. She died on 16 September 1992. He attended the fight at Atlantic City on 11 August but says, 'I felt that my loyalty to my mother in terms of helping to look after her didn't really let me assist Lennox in doing commercial work, and gave me the right to request him to allow me to stand aside and deal with my mother's affairs.'

Lennox employed Levitt as commercial manager because he felt he had an obligation to the man whose fortune had launched his career. 'I don't like turning my back on people who had faith in me at the beginning,' he says. 'I felt he could do a job at the time. But, as we got deeper and deeper into it, people found it very hard to deal with him. He was his own downfall in a way.

'In his own mind he thought he was still in control of everything, and he wouldn't listen to anybody else but me. He was making a lot of plans that I was waiting to come true – like he was going to get this and that deal.

'I'm a person like an elephant – I don't forget. So I just grew sick of it. In a sense, I couldn't deal with a man who really doesn't know too much about boxing and yet who professes that he knows everything about boxing. Basically he was just repeating to me what somebody else had told him. I looked on him as being a potential source of major damage to my career.

'He was there from the beginning of my professional career and he was like a lucky charm for me, because every fight he would make sure he'd come in and wish me good luck. So it didn't really bother me, the fact of him showing up in America. I think it was more his promises, and the power and control he professed to have with other promoters and people in the boxing business, that made my patience run out.

'I still view him as a man with a very thick skin, and a man who will always survive.

'But he's got a beautiful family.'

16

A Truly Dangerous Man

In a world-title eliminator there is no comfort in coming second. Either you win or you're nothing.

When you are one fight from a title shot it's very difficult to convince yourself that it's just another fight. Any man who gets so far and loses has, in a way, been cheated. There is no more bitter a might-have-been than one who almost made it to the top.

The realization that a fighter could be one punch from having all his dreams realized, or from being blown away like confetti in the wind, sets most boxers on edge. In some dressing-rooms on nights when destiny is about to knock, or pass on by, the tension is so heavy and oppressive it could be cut by a cheese-wire.

But on the night of the Razor Ruddock fight, a minute before they started bandaging his hands, Lennox Lewis was sound asleep. He lay on the rubbing-table gently snoring. Ruddock's brother Delroy had done his best to rouse the slumberer by playing loud hip-hop music on a ghetto-blaster, but Lewis slept on. Immobile under a towel, his body teak-hard from weeks of conditioning, he looked like a prizewinning sculpture lying ready to be unveiled. Then Pepe Correa soothed his fighter awake. 'Come on Big Guy,' he whispered – 'It's time to go to work.'

A couple of hours earlier Lennox's manager, Frank Maloney, had been walking the streets of the Royal Borough of Kensington and

Chelsea. He had been to Chelsea Harbour to wish his boxer good luck, and then tried to exercise away his anxiety on an aimless route march around the streets of SW5. In Warwick Road he fell in with the crowd shuffling towards the arena and arrived at Earl's Court long before he had planned to. To fill in time and try to quieten his nervous stomach he ate eight ice-creams.

'When I was boxing I was never on edge,' he says. 'Now I'm a manager it's completely different and I can't relax. Never believe managers who say they feel every punch their boxers take. That's crap – you don't feel any of the punches. What you do is worry instead.

'The team around Lennox can only take him so far – he's on his own in the ring. At a certain stage I have to take a step back. All that's left to me are my thoughts, and I worry.

'When I called on Lennox, he was playing chess and watching television. I sat with him for about forty minutes, chatting about this and that and the laughs we'd had during training. Then I said to him, "You know what you've got to do tonight." He looked at me for a long time and said, "Frank, stop worrying. I'm going out there tonight to do the job. You've got no worries."'

But Lewis's calm conviction did nothing to settle Frank's nerves. With Mike Tyson locked away in an Indiana prison, Ruddock was reckoned to be the most dangerous boxer active in the heavyweight division. For a long time the twenty-eight-year-old Ruddock had been the man to avoid. Even Mike Tyson had sidestepped a championship defence in 1990, cancelling the fight at short notice because of 'pneumonia'. The illness cleared up so quickly that a New York reporter spotted the invalid celebrating in a nightclub a few days later.

After Tyson had lost his title to Buster Douglas, Ruddock met the former champion twice in 1990. The Canadian lasted nineteen frenzied rounds but came out with a double defeat. The first bout ended with a controversial stoppage in the seventh. In the last fight with Iron

Mike, Ruddock battled from the fourth to the twelfth round with a broken jaw which then had to be wired up for six weeks.

When his promoter, Murad Muhammad, visited him in hospital the first thing Ruddock mumbled was, 'I'd have beaten the guy if I'd been an inch and a half taller.' For his part, Tyson described Ruddock's awesome lefthook-cum-uppercut – labelled 'The Smash' – as 'like a kick from a mule'.

So Maloney had reason to be apprehensive. Could Lennox avoid disastrous contact with that Ruddock left smash? The boxer himself had no doubts. As he got up from the rubbing-table, held out his hands to bandaged, and stepped into his cup and his blood-red shorts, he exuded an unshakeable belief in his own supremacy.

It was the early hours of Sunday morning. The fight had been scheduled for 1.00 a.m. to fit in with American prime-time television. Lewis was calm, like a Zen master, filled with sublime confidence that his hour had come. But Lewis was a young man in a hurry. The destruction of Ruddock took him only 3 minutes 46 seconds.

'I don't think my concentration had ever been so fixed or centred before. All the other boxers had put Razor on ice. Bowe didn't want to fight him. Holyfield didn't want to fight him. I think they wanted him in with me so that he could put me out of the reckoning. Their approach to me was, If you want to get somewhere you've got to beat Ruddock. And he was put in the same boat too.

'He is a truly dangerous man, with a good left hook and a good left upper-cut. But he's one-dimensional. I knew that from the times I'd boxed with him in Canada, and I couldn't see a one-dimensional fighter beating me.

'I am a calm guy, because I think things through in my head before I get in the ring. I look at a fight like a chess game or a maths problem – I've got to work out my strategy and tactics. I've got to weigh up my assets and his assets, and work out how my strengths are going to attack his weaknesses. I thought that my tools were too good for him and that he could never beat me as long as I had a good strategy.

'When I first started boxing I used to get butterflies. Some boxers get really sick and throw up before a fight. When I was young I'd get tense, and it used to affect my performance. But, fight after fight, you learn how to relax. Now to me it's just like another day at the office, another shift on the production line. It's nothing to get nervous about.

'Before a fight, I lie down and relax and just put my mind on what's coming up. I concentrate on everything that I've learned and all the things I want to accomplish in the fight. And of course, in my head, I always end up winning. It's like a meditation, a visualization of the fight. I day-dream, positively. And in the middle of it all I usually drop off to sleep.'

Since Ruddock's entourage had arrived in Britain, Maloney had waged a war of nerves on them that would have done credit to spymaster George Smiley. 'When they arrived for the first press conference, I thought to myself, "These people are crazy. They don't know what they're about." When they came into the room, it was like a crowd scene from a Hollywood epic. There were about thirty of them – managers, coaches, bucket-carriers, hangers-on and I don't know what. And I was paying for all their fares. It must have cost more to fly them over here than it cost me to hire the stadium. And they all wanted to take part in the press conference. On the top table it was me and about thirty representatives of Razor Ruddock.

'Then Murad Muhammad stood up and went, "Mr Maloney, welcome to the world of big-time boxing. Enjoy it – it's going to be a very short time for you." I just had to laugh in his face. The arrogance was typical of the Americans. When they come over here they always assume that we haven't got a clue about what we're doing. It was as though the fight was a mere formality. They thought all they had to do was come here, knock over Lennox, pick up their money, and fly back home again.

'They assume because we are quiet we are overawed by a situation. They have a very strange view of the British. They think we're all

"Jolly good show, chaps" and crooked little fingers drinking our Earl Grey tea. The trouble is, none of them have ever been over to South London on a Saturday night.

'What we concentrated on was getting our man ready for the fight, quietly and efficiently. If they wanted to rant and rave, fine – we'd use a bit of kidology to get them stirred up so that they'd rant and rave and unsettle their boxer even more.'

The fight hotel was The White House, near Regent's Park, and it became a magnet for the boxing crowd – managers, promoters, writers, agents and toadies. Mickey Duff used to drop in regularly just to pick up the gossip in the bar. It was hardly the quiet oasis where a boxer can concentrate on the business ahead, but that is where Ruddock stayed in the days before the fight. Lewis was there for a while, but Maloney moved him out to Chelsea Harbour with his fitness coach Courtney Shand and Maloney's brother Eugene, so they could relax during the countdown to the fight.

Then there was the matter of the steroid test. Maybe it was because he was the same nationality as Ben Johnson, but, for whatever reason, Ruddock was very concerned about steroid tests. He has the habit of demanding medical checks to test whether his opponents have artificially built up their physiques by taking steroids. When he fought Mike Tyson, Ruddock demanded a steroid test, but Tyson declined. 'Tyson didn't take it,' claimed Ruddock. 'He paid £25,000 not to take it. I couldn't afford to turn down that money then, but we're in a different position now.'

At the press conference the day before the fight, Ruddock all but foamed at the mouth, threatening he'd be on the next Concorde back to the USA unless Lewis took a steroid test.

Lewis had already given the compulsory blood sample under WBC rules, and told Ruddock, 'You're getting yourself all hyper over nothing – calm your mind.'

Ruddock insisted: 'In my contract it states that I will take a steroid test, an Aids test and all the tests that are necessary. I worked hard to get here, and I don't want anyone coming into the ring and cheating by using steroids.'

An incredulous Lennox demanded, 'Is Razor saying I'm on steroids?' 'No, no, no,' said the wide-eyed Razor. Then it developed into the kind of knock-about theatricals that are employed to squeeze a little more publicity, and hence extra ticket sales, on the eve of a fight.

'Do you want to shut me up?' Lennox demanded – forcing Razor to jump up and appear menacing. There was an element of 'See you behind the bike sheds' about it, but Razor did appear to be nervy and high-strung for a man on the eve of the biggest test of his career. In racing terms, he was a horse that was sweating up and bolting on the way to the starting-gate.

Even then he wouldn't let the subject go away. Razor said to Lennox, 'If you don't have anything to hide, why don't you go pee in a bottle and bring it back here? I'll do the same thing – I have nothing to hide.' It would have made a good picture opportunity for the tabloids, but Lennox declined.

The thoroughness with which the Lewis camp viewed every detail of the fight can by judged by its training schedule. Because the fight was due to take place in the middle of the night, Lennox changed his sleeping pattern and training timetable so that he would be alert and ready for work at the time of the first bell.

'At one o'clock in the morning your body is ready to close down for the night,' says Correa. 'If you're not in bed already, then you should be. In the weeks working up to the Ruddock fight we altered Lennox's body clock so he got used to sleeping at certain hours and training at certain hours. The aim was to make sure that when he went into the ring after midnight Lennox was wide awake and ready to go to work. Ruddock had trained in the afternoon. When the fight started and he needed that big physical effort, his body must have wondered why it was up so late.'

In the small room under the arena, suddenly it was time to go. At long gone midnight there was work to do. Lewis was still iceberg cool and unruffled – almost casual. Earlier they'd had to tell him to hurry up and get his boots on. He really was like a man getting ready for just another day at the office, another shift on the production line.

He huddled in a circle with his cornermen as Pepe Correa intoned a prayer. At the amen, they all punched the air. 'It's time for Lennox to party,' a voice said. 'Let's party!' came the shouted reply. And, protected by a phalanx of minders, the boxer, an island of composure in the maelstrom, danced along the corridor into the biggest fight of his life.

At the ringside Frank Maloney had £5,000 cash on him and was trying to have a wager on the result with Mickey Duff. He claims Duff declined, saying he had bet enough on Ruddock already, but another ringsider struck a bet for £500 with Maloney. 'The noise in the hall was unbelievable,' he says. 'I've never heard anything like the reception Lennox got that night. As soon as he came out it was like a jet taking off – you couldn't hear anything.'

Donovan Ruddock stepped into the spotlight in robes of white satin. He was glistening with sweat, trying to give an impression of jungle fierceness, but he looked more agitated than animated. 'I was just trying to intimidate him, but I guess it didn't work,' he said later.

In the ring he paced about nervously, brandished his fearsome left fist at his former sparring mate from Kitchener, and shouted Moriarty's famous last challenge to Sherlock Holmes – 'Finally, we meet again'. Did Lennox have the answer? 'Yeah, I did,' he said laconically – 'I knocked him down three times.'

Ruddock was first into action, attempting a long left jab to the body which fell short. Lewis got his left jab working and clipped Razor with a long left hook. As Ruddock charged in, both men tangled in a heap on to the bottom rope.

Lennox was happy to hold the centre of the ring jabbing while he moved away from Razor's notorious left hook. Halfway through the round, Lennox's chin was grazed by a Ruddock shot but he was moving out of range and it did no harm.

He was waiting for the opening that Correa had alerted him to during their training sessions in the Pocono Mountains in Pennsylvania. They'd noticed that, every time Ruddock threw a left jab to the body, he left his head open for a right hand over the top. That's a cardinal mistake to make with a tall man who's got a powerful right hand.

With 30 seconds to go to the end of the round, there was a lot of noise coming from Lewis's corner. Courtney Shand was making a sound like 'Bowbowbowbow'. It was a Jamaican slang signal telling Lennox there was half a minute to go. Correa could see that Ruddock's head was open for the shot and was shouting for a right hand from Lennox. From his seat near the corner, another team member, Ollie Dunlap – a former line-backer with the Washington Redskins, whose voice is as piercing as a train whistle – was shouting 'Steal it. Steal it.'

Despite the cacophony of crowd noise, all the messages got through to the boxer. 'I could hear them shouting. I was aware of what they wanted me to do. Then the target opened up for me and I loosed the punch off. To me it wasn't a hard shot – I just rifled it on his temple. It felt like there was a long pause. His legs wobbled with the shock. He took a faltering step. Then he was down,' he says.

'All I was thinking was to get back to the neutral corner so the count could start. The referee was telling me to get back to the corner, and I was saying, "I'm in the corner – start counting." I was wanting him to get the count over. But then the bell went for the end of the round.

'From my stool I looked over to his corner and I could see that his eyes were very wide open, like he was still suffering from shock. That told me he wasn't really there. My corner told me to go out and get right after him, because he was still hurt.'

Ruddock tried to rally in the opening moments of the second, throwing a couple of hopeful lefts. But Lennox forced him into a neutral corner and dropped him with another right to the head. Ruddock was standing after three seconds, but had to take the mandatory count of eight. Again he tried to punch back wildly, but

Lewis finished the job with the mechanical efficiency of a guillotine. Short chopping punches to the head sent Ruddock pitching face first on to the canvas, and referee Joe Cortez waved it over.

'Coming out for the second, I thought I'd give him some of my slo-mo stuff,' says Lennox. 'I come in really slowly and then suddenly start a fast attack. It's something I'd seen in Bruce Lee movies. He starts a movement really slowly and then – Pop! Going slowly seems to put people in a sleep mode – and you surprise them with a sudden strike of speed.

'All of a sudden I felt really strong. I wasn't tired. I had only one object. I could hear the crowd roaring, and that gave me a feeling of power. My only worry was to not get caught with a silly punch. A whole heap of thoughts were going through my mind. I didn't want to leap in too quickly and get caught with a punch like Michael Watson. I've seen it happen in the amateurs a couple of times – someone hurts a guy, rushes in carelessly with his guard down, and gets knocked out. I felt the wind of a couple of his upper-cuts, but I took my time and finished him clinically.

'That was my day – there was no way I was going to lose. I don't think anybody in the world could have beaten me that day.'

There was pandemonium after his hand was raised in victory. Frank Maloney stumbled trying to get into the ring, and someone threw him bodily over the ropes so that he could greet Lennox. 'It was a rugby scrum, with everybody grabbing hold of everybody else,' he says. 'I kept seeing little images, little cameos of people's faces. There was Lennox being lifted up, still looking unruffled by it all. There were cameras poking everywhere. Pepe's glasses glinting in the ring lights. I caught a glimpse of Mickey Duff at the ringside, still looking a bit sour at the result. It was bedlam. I don't know why, but even now I keep choking up every time I think about the fight. You can't explain the pride, the emotion, the great surge of joy that grips you at a moment like that.'

Predictably the newspapers now embraced Lennox as a True Brit.

The *Daily Express* said, 'Perfect fight does Union Jack proud.' In the *Daily Mirror*, Ian Gibb wrote, 'Lennox Lewis can drape himself in the Union Jack and have the keys to the vaults of the Bank of England. He'll be regarded as British as boiled beef and carrots after his quite sensational 3 min 46 secs chopping up of Razor Ruddock.'

Even the xenophobic American press was lavish in its praise. Wallace Matthews of the *New York Newsday* glowed, 'It almost seemed as if Lewis had wiped out 93 years of English heavyweight futility in 3 minutes and 46 seconds.'

After the ring had cleared a little, Lennox had some words of comfort for his opponent. 'He asked me to win the title for him now that he'd lost the chance, and I promised that I would,' Lennox recalls. 'Since then I've seen Razor three times and told him I wanted to speak to him, but he never made the approach to get in touch. I wanted to tell him that he should still keep boxing. I've heard things through the grapevine that he's depressed and that he's not going to box any more. I think that's a waste. Just because you lose doesn't mean that's the end of your life – that's the way I look at it. It wouldn't have been the end of mine.'

Asked what Evander Holyfield would have to bring in the ring with him to deal with Lennox, Lou Duva, the champion's trainer, said, 'How about a shotgun? And maybe a machine-gun for luck? I always thought Lennox would win, but never did I think he would wipe out Ruddock just like that.

'It may have taken you Brits nearly a hundred years to come up with this guy, but I've got to say he fought a super fight. Lennox Lewis has got everything it takes.'

At Earls Court Arena the old campaigner George Foreman summed up Lennox's prospects by clicking one of his huge fingers against a leathery thumb. 'Lennox Lewis,' he said, 'can be champ just like that.' The next two weeks were filled with eager speculation about Lewis's upcoming title shot. 'Roll on April and watch out

America,' said Jeff Powell in the *Daily Mail*. 'At long last, Britain has found a heavyweight who is finger-snapping good.'

An exultant Lewis was soon brought back down to earth after his stunning victory over Ruddock. When he and his running-companion/driver/minder Eugene Maloney walked out to the car park, they discovered that someone had stolen their Jaguar.

Worse was to follow. Thirteen days later Riddick Bowe became the new heavyweight champion when he beat Holyfield over twelve rounds. Straight away Lewis's chance to win the title outright was put on hold. The last man Bowe wanted to meet in his first defence was the man who had robbed him of the Olympic gold medal at Seoul in 1988.

17

The Mafia and the Monarch

They say he's difficult. They say he's a jumped-up little know-all. They say he's feeding his champion easy opponents. They say that in negotiations he's insufferable. They say a lot more about him that's unprintable.

Frank Maloney says every word of this is true. Even the unprintable stuff.

The 'he' Frank is referring to is Rock Newman.

On 13 November 1992 Lennox and Frank Maloney were at the Tomas and Mack Center in Las Vegas when Rock Newman's protégé Riddick Bowe won the world heavyweight title from Evander Holyfield. Lennox was at the ringside as guest analyst for HBO, and Frank did the inter-round summaries for Sky TV from its commentary point.

'In my mind I wanted Holyfield to win,' says Maloney, 'because I knew that if Bowe won we had a problem.'

They did. The agreement signed by the four men who took part in the mini-tournament to settle the heavyweight succession – Holyfield, Bowe, Lewis, Ruddock – was not a binding contract but a letter of intent that the winner of Bowe–Holyfield would meet the winner of the Lewis–Ruddock 'fight for the right'.

Even before Bowe won the title, Newman was hinting that the first defence might be not against Lewis but against George Foreman in

China, a rather easier pay-day. After all his scuffling to get Bowe the title and the open-sesame to a fortune, Newman wanted to avoid Bowe losing a difficult first defence.

Eugene Roderick Newman, forty-one, had picked up Bowe after his Olympic defeat by Lennox Lewis, when Butch Lewis (no relation), for whom Newman worked as a spokesman, chose not to pursue the silver-medallist. After the loss in Seoul, a depressed Bowe, who was married and had two children to support, contemplated giving up boxing to join the army. Newman, a former car salesman, counsellor at Howard University and radio talk-show host in Washington, had other ideas. He persuaded Bowe that he was championship class and managed him to an impressive professional record of 32 wins, 0 defeats, 27 knockouts. It was a struggle. Several times he had to put up money to pay opponents just to keep his man busy. In January 1990 he even sold his 1988 BMW for $25,000 to keep Bowe solvent.

Newman was fiercely protective of his asset. Once he shoved a rival manager, Marc Roberts, during a live TV interview. On another occasion he had climbed on to the ring apron to wrestle with Elijah Tillery when Tillery kicked Bowe several times during a bout in 1991. Having got to the top of the greasy pole, he wasn't going to let Maloney knock him off first go.

The tone of the relationship between the two camps was set as Bowe was leaving the ring after his victory over Holyfield. He spied Lewis at the ringside and went across to face him. There was an exchange of insults through the ropes, because Lewis had tipped Holyfield to win. For a while it looked as though big-fight referee Joe Cortez would have some unexpected overtime.

It got worse at the post-fight press conference, where Lewis and Maloney were invited up to the top table by Newman. Lewis, who was wearing his hair in a small pony-tail on the nape of his neck, tried to compliment the new champion on his unanimous points win. 'You're so kind,' Bowe mocked. 'I've got sisters who could whup you.' As the exasperated Lewis and Maloney stood up to leave, Bowe shouted after the boxer, 'Get your great feet south. I like your pony-tail, Lennox, you big faggot!'

Looking back Lennox says, 'It was silly and undignified, but I suppose he was still fired up from the fight. I'd predicted a Holyfield win, and obviously Bowe saw what I had said in all the papers and it bugged him. I wanted Holyfield to win because I knew if he didn't Bowe would be reluctant to box me, and that's the way it turned out exactly.

'I suppose Bowe felt some kind of strength after his win and came over to me at the ringside and there was a confrontation. He was pointing at me saying, "Yeah, you're next." And I said, "Yeah, bring it on." Then he gets out of the ring and walks down the line, and I stepped back because I thought he was going back to the dressing-room. I was still wearing the headphones from the broadcast. But instead of walking by he put his face right in mine and said, "I thought you were cool."

'I didn't know what he was talking about, but I said to him, "Why don't you fight me?" He said, "Yeah, I'll fight you." I told him, "I'll knock you out," and that got him pretty mad. I was serious at the time. Lots of things were going through my mind very fast, visualizing what could happen.

'But then I thought, "This is a bit silly." I couldn't see myself punching him in the face and knocking him out after he'd just gone twelve rounds with Holyfield. That's what I felt like doing, though, because I don't allow people to come up to me like that.

'We're both gladiators in our sport. We've both got egos. I think it could have come to a fight there and then. But I realized a lot of people were watching and it just wouldn't be the right thing. So at that point I kept my cool, and eventually he went off. A lot of people praised me for that and said it was the right thing to do.

'Afterwards, when we were at the press conference, I congratulated him again on being the new champion and he started going on about his sisters being able to beat me and me being a faggot. He made a fool of himself, basically, and it took me back to the way he had acted at the 1988 Olympics. His team-mates there were saying to me, "Beat him up. I hope you knock him out. He's a big mouth."

'In a way it was a pity for him, because he spoiled his own press conference. He was the champion, that was his time – not the time to make a fool of himself. When he began to insult me, it crossed my mind, "Should I rush him and punch him in the head?" But then I thought the best thing to do was leave quietly, with some dignity.

'But it did prove to me that I get to him, that I affect him. I'm sure it must bug him, because every time they speak about his championship they speak about me in the same breath and ask him when he is going to fight me. I'm sure he's sick and tired of hearing my name by now.'

That was the prelude to months of diversions from Newman as he sought to match his man against almost anyone but the legitimate contender. At one stage he even talked about staging Bowe's first defence during half-time of the Superbowl contest on NBC on 31 January 1993. The trouble is, the half-time lasts for 20 minutes, while a twelve-round contest lasts 48. To make television-scheduling sense, Bowe would have needed an opponent he was certain to finish off in the time allowed. 'That shows you how serious the fight would have been,' grumbles Maloney. (Given that his first two ludicrous defences lasted a total of just 3 minutes 36 seconds, Bowe should have time to dispatch four or five mildewed challengers for his WBA/IBF titles during the half-time of next year's Superbowl.)

The mutual antagonism between the two camps led to a winter of publicity stunts involving the extravagant pantomime of Frank Maloney's chicken costumes and Rock Newman's dustbin theatricals with the discarded WBC belt. With all this piquant name-calling, the showdown between Lewis and Bowe is in danger of becoming the yeti of world boxing – a creature of vague rumour and wild stories, but with no real evidence for its existence.

Negotiations have gone on, but the hostilities that have broken out at the end of them have been not a battle of fists between the boxers but a war of words between their respective managers. The HBO TV company wants to put up most of the money for the title-unification bout everyone wants to see. There is something like $32 million in the kitty. The arguments are about how to divide it up.

The first offer made by Newman to Maloney at the end of last year was $3 million for Lewis to fight Bowe. This was unacceptable to the British team, since it meant that Bowe would pick up 90 per cent of the purse and Lewis only 10 per cent. 'Newman was taking liberties. If it went to purse offers, Lennox would get 25 per cent at least,' says Maloney. The next suggestion was $2 million to Lewis to fight on the undercard of Bowe's first WBA/IBF title defence (not the one during the Superbowl interval). This was in return for a promise that Lewis would be offered Bowe's second title defence. 'They've broken their word to us once after the Ruddock fight,' says Maloney. 'Why should we trust them again?'

In February there was a meeting at HBO's Manhattan offices, attended by, among others, Newman, Maloney and Dan Duva. Newman, wearing a large cowboy hat and a flowing overcoat, suggested a purse of $10 million for Lewis, out of which Lewis would have to pay Duva $5 million — which Newman owed Duva from the Holyfield–Bowe promotion. 'I told him that was totally unacceptable,' says Maloney. 'It was like buying a house and then expecting someone else to pick up the mortgage on it.'

Another formula was that both fighters would get $5 million, the winner would get an additional jackpot from the $32 million, and the loser only the addition of training expenses. From this developed Newman's gambler's option of the winner taking all the purse from the $32 million gross. The loser would get virtually nothing, bar his training expenses.

Maloney told Newman he would have to consult his boxer and get back to him. 'Because we're a team and I don't take decisions on behalf of Lennox without consulting him, I told Newman I'd have to put the winner-take-all suggestion to Lennox and call him back,' says

Maloney. 'Lennox was eager to go ahead and do it. The next day I faxed our acceptance to Newman's office. Since then I haven't had a word back from him. He seems to have gone dead on the idea.

'To be honest, I don't think Rock Newman has any intention of letting Bowe meet Lennox – at least not for a while. What he's doing is trying to create a smokescreen to suggest that we're being greedy, or that Lewis is trying to duck Bowe, when we say it's the other way round.

'I think he's just playing games. Newman might start serious negotiations about a fight after Bowe has fought a few more no-hopers and earned lots more money, but for the moment's he's just play-acting. That man tests your sanity. Before long, Bowe will have lost so much credibility he'll need a fight with Lennox. The next time we get round a table the negotiations will start at 50–50.'

So the big showdown could yet happen. One day, maybe. 'Don't rule out the summer to autumn of 1994,' says Maloney.

'I'd be happy to fight Riddick, any time, any place,' says Lennox. 'I've proved to the world I can beat him, and he certainly holds no fears for me. My only worry is that each time he's defended his title he's gone into the ring looking flabby. He's putting on weight and looks out of condition. What could happen is that someone else will beat him before I can get to him. I wouldn't want that, because I want to beat him first and unify the titles.'

Maloney's titanic struggles with Newman were soon to pale into insignificance. The WBC denied Lennox a voluntary defence (where he would be able to chose his own opponent) and ruled that his first challenger should be the official number one, Tony Tucker. Since the thirty-four-year-old ex-champion was controlled by the egregious Don King, Maloney soon found himself coming to verbal blows with Mr Thousand Volts himself, the former numbers racketeer and convict.

Lennox wanted to stage the first defence of his title in Britain. 'After ninety-four years without a world champion at heavyweight, I thought that it was only right that we should try to stage the fight at home,' says Lennox. 'But there were practical reasons too. I thought it would be risky fighting in America in a promotion controlled by Don King. Under him I thought that anything that could happen, would happen. Murphy's Law would come into effect. I'd seen it before, where boxers have beaten their opponent yet not gotten the fight. I didn't want that to happen to me, so I was willing to take less money for the fight to come to London.'

So Frank Maloney went to Mexico with the mission to win the purse bid and bring the fight to London. He and Dan Duva each put in a bid, and were astounded when Don King won the sealed auction with an offer of $12 million. Since Mike Tyson's imprisonment, King had been pushed to the fringes of heavyweight boxing. This was his throw to try to win back some of his lost power and maybe, while he was at it, to influence the WBC champion, Lennox Lewis, to throw in his hand with him.

'It was an astronomical bid, and we were staggered by it,' says Maloney. 'We couldn't see how he was going to guarantee such big money for the fight and make a profit from it.'

The bid meant that Lennox would be taking $9 million from his first title defence. Maloney had the job of ringing to tell him the bad news. 'I phoned Lennox and said, "Look, I don't know how to tell you this. The news is good and bad." He said, "How come?" So I told him, "We lost the bid, so the fight can't take place in Britain. But you're going to break all records for your first defence and get $9 million.

'He said, "That wasn't supposed to happen. I wasn't really worried about the money – I wanted to fight in London."'

Maloney was still slightly in shock from the size of the winning purse bid, and from the experience of his first major confrontation with Don King. 'He would frighten the life out of you if you didn't know what to expect. He bombs into every room and starts waving his arms and shouting at the top of his voice. His voice gets louder and louder, and he preaches a mixture of Shakespearian quotes, poetry and verses from the Bible at you. When he was in prison he must have learned the dictionary of quotations by heart,' he says.

'The thing is, it's all nonsense. He's like a preacher talking gibberish. He takes you round the world on a tour of quotations from literature and the Bible, then he brings you back to the same place and you're no wiser than when you started out.

'Half the time I don't think he even knows what he's talking about himself. My tactic is to listen and nod and say, "I've taken note of what you've said and I'll get back to you."'

Lennox's training camp was at Hilton Head, on the coast of South Carolina. In the first days of his six-week stint there he damaged his right hand while sparring. He flew to New York to see a specialist, who told him he had split the extender tendon in the knuckle of his little finger. It would need an operation eventually, but as long as he nursed it the fight could go ahead.

'It badly affected my training. I couldn't put in all the necessary rounds, and for five weeks I had to spar with one hand all the time. I couldn't work the heavy bag either, so it spoiled my whole training regimen,' says Lennox.

'It was a psychological mountain for me. In my mind I hadn't trained as I should. I wasn't ready. I didn't know whether the hand would last through twelve rounds of hard punching. That was another thing on my mind.

'It was hard mentally on me. It was a very important fight for me. If I lost my title at the first defence, I would be humiliated. It would be a big blow to my pride. If I cancelled, there was a lot of money involved. So I said no to a postponement, because I believed I could win using all my other assets.'

The training team of Pepe Correa, assistant trainer Harold Knight and fitness coach Courtney Shand had to get Lennox fighting fit without damaging the knuckle further, and without the press and public getting wind of his injury.

'It was hard on Lennox,' says Courtney Shand. 'Every night he had to sleep with his fist in a bucket of iced water – not the best way of getting a good night's rest. Then people started getting inquisitive about why he wasn't sparring much, and we had to talk our way out of that. If any strangers were about, Lennox used to go around with his hands in his pockets so that people couldn't see that his right hand was swollen.'

'You have to take your hat off to Lennox in that fight,' says Correa. 'His hand was hurting him, but he refused to pull out. There were days when I had to bullshit the public and make excuses for why he was only using his left hand in sparring.

'I asked him if he really wanted to go ahead. He said, "I want this fight, and I'll give it my all." But I'll be honest – he went into it only 45 per cent ready. But he told me he could still win it in spite of the bad hand, and that's all I wanted to hear.'

Meanwhile Frank was having problems with Don King. Having put up $12 million, the promoter was anxious to recoup as much as possible and was selling the fight hard. He wanted to involve Lewis in a series of promotions, interviews and media events. Maloney was happy to fulfil all his contractual obligations, but didn't want his injured boxer overburdened with public appearances. Mr King was not pleased. Among the nicer things he said about Frank was, 'Maloney's a mental midget, a little weasel, a treacherous snake in the grass. When I am near him I feel like a porcupine 'cos of all the arrows in my back.'

Maloney's response was to say, 'Thank you very much, Mr King, for making me famous.'

The great pontificator made no attempts to disguise his ambition to entice Lennox away from his manager. In a scurrilous open letter headed 'The Indiscretions of Frank Maloney. Vicious, Stupid or Both????', he attacked Frank in lurid terms that would have earned a fortune in damages if published in Britain.

The letter was addressed 'Dear Lennox, Family and Genuine

Friends'. It rambled on in typical King style for four pages, but the message was clear: sign with me. It said, 'Lennox, you are a potentially awesome heavyweight boxer. But you are being held back by this mental midget, this pugilistic pygmy, named Frank Maloney. You can't fly a multimillion dollar airplane properly when you are being guided by a ten-cent control tower.'

But Lennox was immune to all of King's wooing. King had tried to lure the boxer into his camp several times before, but the boxer had resisted. Even now he had written into his contract for the fight a clause stating that he would not meet King alone.

'His pursuit of me was very blatant,' says Lennox, 'but there is no way I would ever sign to him. If you just take a look at history it speaks for itself and warns you about him. With Mike Tyson he was a sweet-talker, but he didn't care about him enough to keep him straight in ethical ways, and he helped destroy him by that neglect. There are lots of boxers down the line that have been hurt by King in lots of ways.

'I know you sometimes have to deal with these guys as a professional, but I certainly wouldn't go with him. If I see him at a weigh-in or a fight he'll make an approach. One time he said to me, "Let's get together and make some money." I just smiled and said, "Hiya, Don. How are you doing?" He's been tapping me for years, but I know too much about him and his methods.

'He's got a way with words, and he's a motivator. He can talk you out of your socks if you listen to him. He fascinates me, as a study, in the way Roger Levitt fascinated me, but I've always resisted his approaches. I mean, look at his names – Don and King. Two very powerful names – the Mafia and the monarch. Interesting. Every time he has the chance he tries to get to me. But I say no.

'Like I said once before, "How can you trust a man who can talk for five minutes and you can't understand a sentence." '

Lennox's opponent at the Thomas and Mack Centre in Las Vegas on 8 May 1993 was thirty-three-year-old Tony Tucker, the former

IBF champion, who had lost only one of his fifty fights, and that was to Mike Tyson in 1987. At one stage in his career his father, Robert, sold off shares in Tony to as many buyers as he could find. Business was brisk, and he managed to sell off 120 per cent of his son – with the result that poor Tony saw little or nothing of his purse money. He found God, and came to regard Don King as the saviour of his career on earth – as no doubt would anyone whose father's maths was that bad.

Tucker was built like a heavyweight but boxed with the speed, fluency and variation of a middleweight. Though Tyson had beaten him he hadn't knocked him down. Tucker was regarded as the toughest man in the rankings, having delivered more KOs than Lewis had had wins.

Tucker's camp was led by the notorious Panama Lewis, a King crony from Philadelphia who is banned from officiating as a cornerman by forty-eight of the forty-nine boxing commissions in the USA. His crime was to remove the protective stuffing from the gloves of his fighter Luis Resto before a bout with a boxer called Billy Collins at Madison Square Garden a decade ago. Collins was so badly maimed he had to retire.

The lurid promotional video for the fight showed Tucker and Lewis wrapped in their respective national flags, with Tucker hyperventilating, 'God may save the Queen, but nobody's gonna save Lennox Lewis.'

At a hysterical pre-fight press conference, Tucker had sung that he would make Lennox fall down like London Bridge. But it was he who was knocked over – twice. In the third round a long straight right from Lennox sent the challenger sprawling against the ropes for the first knockdown in his career. Lewis sent Tucker down again early in the ninth, but seemed to run out of steam trying to finish him off.

At the finish Lennox was well ahead on points and coasting. He won on all three score cards – 116–112, 118–111 and 117–111 – but at times he had looked tentative, and it was obvious that his lack of preparation and the problem with his hand had affected his performance.

'You had two counter-punchers in the ring together, which was never going to give you a great fight,' says Pepe Correa. 'But he put Tucker down twice – which is more than anyone else has ever done. Given the training problems, it was a magnificent result and a credit to Lennox's tremendous will-power.'

'I know that if I didn't do anything silly I had it won long before the end,' says Lennox. 'Frank came round to the corner and told me not to take any risks, which is why some people thought I had got tired and faded after the ninth. With two good hands I would have easily knocked him out.

'In the end I was just glad to win and get away from Don King as quickly as possible. But the fans were magnificent. There were lots of British supporters there, and they gave me great encouragement. I could hear them all the way through. We were all part of a little history being made. That night I became the first Briton to win a heavyweight title fight in the USA for ninety-six years.'

Maloney had shrewdly insisted that his boxer's $9 million was to be paid in a lump sum, guaranteed by a letter of credit, so King was left crying all the way to the bank – with his man well beaten, Lewis contemptuously resisting his overtures, and an estimated loss of $3.8 million on the promotion.

The proudest man at the ringside was Lennox's first coach, Arnie Boehm. He and his wife, Verna, had been guests of Lewis in Las Vegas for the week of the fight. 'I'd been saying for years that Lennox would win the world title, so it was a special joy to be there when he proved in that first defence that he was a worthy champion,' says Arnie, 'I told him I hoped my other dream for him came true – that he invests his money wisely, gets out of the game, marries a nice girl, and has a fine bunch of kids.

'I said that, when he'd raised the fine bunch of kids, I'd volunteer to coach his boys.'

18

History in the Making

Humidity is high. Only a few minutes after dawn on a day that's already too hot for vigorous exercise, the morning has the look and feel of a warm, damp flannel. Yet the joggers are out on Pebble Mill Drive.

They cut across the grass verge and down a path that leads to a golf-course in suburban Maryland. They could be three businessmen out for a run before setting off for a day in the office – until you notice their pace. A man with half an eye – which is all anybody could be expected to have open at this hour of the morning – should have clocked that they are far too fit to be mere exercise freaks.

It's the start of a yet another day of relentless training for Lennox Lewis. The dot of 5.15 means an 8-mile cross-country run as he prepares for the serious business of his world-title showdown with Frank Bruno.

Boxing is a harsh mistress, and one of her cruellest rules is having to get up to punish your body when it feels like turning over and having another hour in bed. But this is merely routine for Lennox. Forty minutes later he returns, scarcely ruffled, his buddies – Courtney Shand and Eugene Maloney – trailing in his wake. He has beaten them again. It's business as usual.

The American writer Nelson Algren in *What Every Young Man Should Know* once wrote, 'Never eat at a place called Mom's. Never play cards with a man named Doc. And never lie down with a woman who's got more troubles than you.' A fourth piece of advice can now be added to the list: never try to compete with Lennox Lewis. Not at anything. The man is a self-made, painstaking, thoroughly shrewd, psychologically diabolical winner. At everything.

He strides up the path to the house on Pebble Beach Drive that serves as quarters for his six weeks at training camp. Competitive edge whetted by the run, he is ready for a second challenge. On the kitchen table a chessboard is set out with the pieces already in place for the first game of the day. Having beaten the opposition at running, he will now checkmate them before breakfast.

Many people have commented on the similarity between boxing and chess. The sports writer George Plimpton said, 'No sport (other than boxing) exists in which one's attention is directly focused on the opposition for such a long time – except perhaps chess – so that matters of pyschological pressure are certainly in effect.' In *On Boxing*, Joyce Carol Oates wrote, 'Boxers, like chess players, must be able to think on their feet, must be able to improvise in mid-fight, so to speak.'

Lennox agrees that sedentary chess can be as ruthless as his own bloody profession. 'You only have to hear the tone that creeps into people's voices when they say "Check" to realize it's just as competitive as boxing,' he says, 'In both you are responsible for your actions. If you make a bad move you are punished. Chess helps sharpen a boxer's mind. It shows you the value of clear thinking, strategy and daring to be best. In chess and boxing you are always having to admit that you could do better, so you need to concentrate your mind and train to improve.'

At his retreat in Maryland – just a commuter ride from The White House – Lennox has been planning his strategy for the destruction of Frank Bruno. The fight at Cardiff Arms Park in the early hours of 2 October is billed as history in the making, the match the British public all want. That's not just boxing hype. As John Morris, secretary of the British Boxing Board of Control, says, 'This is without doubt the most important heavyweight contest ever to take place in Britain. Lewis won back a share in the world title for us after a wait of ninety-four years. Now we can enjoy another illustrious event. When Lennox and Frank face each other in Cardiff it will be the first time that two British-born boxers have ever met to fight for a world heavyweight crown. The wonderful certainty is that, whoever wins, we will still have a British heavyweight champion of the world the next morning.'

Lewis is preparing himself for the contest with the relentlessness of a chainsaw. 'I've never seen his mind and energy so concentrated,' says Frank Maloney. 'It's like a rerun of his training for Razor Ruddock. He really wants to get at Bruno and blast him off the scene.'

Lewis has put his WBC belt up for grabs against a man who has twice failed to win the heavyweight championship. Apart from the crucial business of the title, however, there are other important issues on the agenda.

'I want to settle once and for all who is the best boxer in Britain,' says Lennox. 'Because Bruno's a character who's been on the scene for a while, and had a couple of title shots, lots of misguided people think he's still the best heavyweight we've got. But he hasn't been the best for years.

'Bruno is a national hero for being a loser. I want to be a national hero for being a winner. It's as simple as that. I want to change the British attitude to failure. In some areas we've got so used to failure that it's all we expect. There's an impression that somehow losing is better, more worthy. But winning is even better. I think we all need to be more upbeat and focused about winning.'

Eight miles from the chessboard, along George Palmer Highway, past the shabby trailer tempting motorists with the sign 'Home Boy Hot Crabs', is the Sugar Ray Leonard gym. There, under stark neon lights, Lennox sweats through his training routine watched by benches full of gnarled old-timers and neighbourhood kids. It's an awesome sight. After an hour, entranced by the big man flailing the speed ball, the creak of ropes, the rhythms of skipping and the warm thwack of leather on headguard, they are goggle-eyed at his artistry. They haven't seen anyone this sharp since Sugar Ray himself trained here.

The whole sweaty, thrilling performance is orchestrated by a buzzer measuring 3-minute rounds, 30 seconds' warning to the end of the round, and 1 minute of rest. Lennox's performance is so good there should be an ovation at the end of every round, not just a buzzer.

In a game where most of the heroes have faces like dug-up roads, Lennox is the handsome exception. At 6 feet 5 inches and 15 st. 6 lb. he is built like a granite fortification. He is not muscle-bound like some heavyweights – there is a litheness and grace about him that hints of Mohammad Ali at his floating-butterfly best. He exudes a sense of contained strength and calm confidence. Everyone in the gym from the most humble bucket-carrier to the man himself is rock-solid about what will happen in Cardiff. As trainer Pepe Correa has it: 'There is only one result: Bruno loses.'

'It should be a good fight, because both men are fit and dedicated boxers,' he says. 'But Bruno is a lumbering bus, and my big guy is like a fine-tuned grand-prix racing machine. No matter how much they try to disguise his shortcomings, Bruno will always be the same boxer. There is nothing new he can learn at this stage of his career. He will be the same Frank Bruno who always gets beaten by good fighters. All the good fighters he has met have whipped him. On 2 October it happens again. *Déjà vu.*'

Assistant trainer Harold Knight, who went fifteen rounds to lose a narrow decision against Rocky Lockridge for the junior-lightweight title in 1988, is responsible for ensuring that the sparring partners give the champion a hard time. They are a phlegmatic, softly spoken crew: four towering black men – Sherman Griffin, Cleveland Woods, Ray Annis and Julius Francis – plus the Pole Andrei Golota, an

Olympic bronze-medallist. Every morning Harold exercises them on Maryland University golf-course. They stampede round the eighteen holes as heavy and purposeful as beef cattle. 'They are all fit and strong,' says Harold. 'We've picked them so they can duplicate Bruno's style for us. They're all like him, except they're all much faster than he is.

'One of Lennox's strengths is that he can adapt to any situation quickly. You only have to tell him a new move once and he's got it. It takes him less than a round or two to figure out his sparring partners. That's why we have to keep changing them.'

In the past Lennox has wasted sparring partners with the efficiency of a scatter-gun. At Hilton Head, training for the Tucker fight, Ruben 'Hurricane' Hadley got so fed up at being constantly belted that he bit Lewis on the shoulder. But, though Lennox keeps tagging them, these sparring partners use more orthodox methods to fight back.

Ollie Dunlap, the camp coordinator, is an amiable bear of a man with a grizzled beard that looks like a sprinkling of rock salt. 'Lennox will win this one like he's won all the others, because defeat is something he doesn't even consider. Of all the sportsman I've ever worked with, his will to win stands out as quite extraordinary. He's a world champion, he's made millions, and yet he's still hungry to learn and improve himself. Other boxers, once they've won a title, sometimes act as though they know it all and no one can teach them anything. But Lennox is still humble enough to seek advice. He wants to be a great champion. He wants to get better. That's why I don't think we've seen the best of him yet – not by a long way.'

In a reflective moment back over the chessboard, Lennox talks down some of the hype about the fight with Bruno. 'I am going to beat him,' he says calmly, 'But it's not a grudge thing – I don't hate him. Frank is a nice popular guy. Everybody likes him. I just think his time has come to retire. He belonged to the '80s, and I'm the man of this decade.

'We met a few years back, away from the limelight, when I was on holiday in Jamaica. I was on a moped when I heard this great shout and it was Frank. He was on his way to see his grandmother in Negril.

'I said to him, "Don't take too much notice of the things you read about our rivalry in the papers. None of it is meant." And he said, "Yeah – it's only business, isn't it?'"

Lennox's brother Dennis's father, Rupert Daries, is masseur to Frank Bruno, and Lennox chuckles over the dilemma Rupert finds himself in. 'He likes me, and he likes Frank too. So that leaves him with the problem of who to support on the night of the fight,' he says. 'I suppose he'll end up shouting for Frank, because he's his boss. But I hope he'll be cheering for me too when I win.'

Lennox walks, talks and thinks boxing, but his face doesn't show it. The only blemish to his sharp good looks is a small scar on his forehead, caused when a sporting-gun recoiled.

'There are some boxers who have flattened noses and cauliflower ears, but not every boxer. Look at Sugar Ray Leonard. Look at me. It annoys me when people automatically assume that boxers are stupid, that we can't talk about anything that happens outside the ring or the gym. Fighters have to think inside the ring, so why should people be surprised if we think outside it and talk about world events, read books or take an interest in chess?'

The tight-knit team that Fran Maloney has built around Lewis gives the boxer the kind of unswerving support that monks give to their father superior. During the boxer's training retreat, everyone else sweats through his own purgatory of exercise. From assistant security man Harry Maneh to Frank Maloney, they go through a softer, gentler echo of the boxer's daily grind.

The sight of Maloney pounding up and down the terracing at Maryland University's Byrd Stadium prompts one onlooker to suggest that Frank should make a boxing comeback and challenge Mickey Duff on the Cardiff undercard. He declines the offer.

One night, to break the monotony of training, there is an outing to

Lorten State Penitentiary in Virginia to see a prison boxing match. Riddick Bowe, who lives a few miles down the road, had declined the invitation to attend – like he declines the invitations to fight Lewis. In Bowe's absence, Lennox milks the applause and wins over a whole new bunch of fans. 'I'd like to best Bowe right here and now,' he says to wild cheering. With a thousand desperate faces – some of them, the prison cross-dressers, all rouged and primped for the fight night – it is like a scene from a Hogarth print of the stews and jails of eighteenth-century London. Alternatively, 'it's just like the ringside at Atlantic City', says one of the sparring partners. The Pole has to be told in slow-mo English that, no, Lorten isn't a mixed jail. There is a delay before the first fight. One of the inmates actually shouts the old joke 'Hurry up – I've only got forty-nine years.'

But, even on his night off, Lennox's thoughts are never far away from the most important item on his current agenda. 'I can't wait to get to Cardiff,' he says. 'It's going to be a historic night, and I'm looking forward to it.'

And who's going to win? 'The Englishman,' he replies. 'Me.'

APPENDIX I

Fighting Weights
and Boxing Authorities

The fighting weights (in pounds) currently recognized by the four boxing authorities are: straw, 105; junior fly, 108; fly, 112; junior bantam, 115; bantam, 118; junior feather, 122; feather, 126; super-feather, 130; light, 135; junior welter, 140; welter, 147; junior middle, 154; middle, 160; super-middle, 168; light-heavy, 175; cruiser, 195; heavy, unlimited. (Some of the mini-weights are ludicrously close together. Drinking a cup of tea before the weigh-in could make the difference between a boxer fighting at one weight or another. A tea with two sugars could put him up two divisions.)

The era of eight undisputed world champions may have given fans better value, but the golden age was tarnished. Big boxing promoters, the New York Athletic Association and the monopolistic International Boxing Club (IBC), controlled by a gangster named Frankie Carbo, carved up who fought whom. Boxers who lacked the right connections were kept away from lucrative champion status.

'Ageless' Archie Moore – 'The Einstein of boxing', according to fellow toiler Tony Anthony – was thirty-nine years old before he got (and won) a world-title fight in 1952. Between 1949 and 1959 the IBC of New York staged 99 per cent of all championship fights. The Supreme Court ruled that such activity gave the IBC 'an odorous monopoly background' that was 'feared in the boxing world.'

New boxing authorities began to spring up in the 1960s to the approval of managers and boxers who distrusted the established system. At the same time, television companies realized that title fights were big ratings winners. As there were so many rival channels, the more titles to fill competing schedules the better.

The World Boxing Association (WBA) was formed in 1962 by a group of Panamanians. It developed from the National Boxing Association (NBA), established in 1921 by other US states where boxing was popular, who were disgruntled at the monopoly held by New York.

A year later, on St Valentine's Day 1963, the World Boxing Council (WBC) was established with the help of several national associations – including the British Boxing Board of Control – who were unhappy at the WBA's assumption of world control. The new body also received support from the boxing department of the New York Athletic Association – so in a different guise it renewed the rivalry of the 1920s between it and the NBA.

Since the WBC is based in Mexico City and the WBA in Maracay, Venezuela – neither place a haven of probity and fair play – there's almost a guarantee of wrangling over titles and rankings.

In 1983 the American-based International Boxing Federation (IBF) was formed by people disaffected with the WBA and WBC. The World Boxing Organization (WBO) owed its formation in the late 1980s to the isolation of South African sportsmen during the apartheid era. It was founded by a South African boxing referee, Stan Christodoulou, to get 'world title' fights for his countrymen.

More recently the set-up has become even more complex. Beau Williford, a Louisiana manager who cannot get his boxers the fights he wants, has started the Universal Boxing Association (UBA). Elsewhere in America, the World Boxing Federation (WBF) has been created to boost status and prizes for Australian boxers.

'There is only one God,' as Frank Bruno once pointed out, 'but not necessarily only one heavyweight champion.' This proliferation of initials and contenders is good for television channels, which can tempt viewers with an average of 130 world-title fights a year, but it is confusing for the public. There was an apt cartoon in Bert Randolph Sugar's *Boxing Illustrated* in July 1990. It showed a ring crowded with champions who had just been introduced by a harassed announcer during those interminable pre-fight preliminaries. The announcer is apologizing to the crowd: 'And so unfortunately, fight fans, after all the ring introductions of all the current champions of the various sanctioning organizations . . . we won't have time for the main event.'

Years ago you didn't need much gumption to recite the eight champions of the world. But now you need the IQ of a member of Mensa to recollect that Myung-Woo-Yuh is the WBA champion at 108 lb.

APPENDIX 2

Lennox Lewis's
Professional Ring Career

FIGHT ONE

DATE   27 June 1989
VENUE   Royal Albert Hall, London
WEIGHT   16 st. 7 lb.
OPPONENT   Al Malcolm, Birmingham – 15 st. 5 lb.
RESULT   KO 2
SUMMARY   Eager to impress, debutant Lewis floors Malcolm for eight with a left hook in the first, then repeats the dose after 19 seconds of round two to make the Midland-area champ take the full count.

FIGHT TWO

DATE   21 July 1989
VENUE   Convention Hall, Atlantic City, New Jersey
WEIGHT   16 st. 1 lb.
OPPONENT   Bruce Johnson, Ohio – 13 st. 10 lb.
RESULT   TKO 2
SUMMARY   His American debut, on the card of the Tyson–Williams title fight, sees Lewis overpower the journeyman Johnson for a second-round stoppage.

FIGHT THREE

DATE 25 September 1989
VENUE National Sports Centre, Crystal Palace
WEIGHT 16 st. 10½ lb.
OPPONENT Andy Gerrard, Risca, Wales – 16 st. 1 lb.
RESULT TKO 4
SUMMARY Lewis paces himself for three rounds until right-handers in the fourth result in the Welshman being rescued when helpless under fire.

FIGHT FOUR

DATE 10 October 1989
VENUE City Hall, Hull
WEIGHT 16 st. 8 lb.
OPPONENT Steve Garber, Bradford – 16 st.
RESULT KO 1
SUMMARY An overwhelming show as Lewis floors his opponent twice before knocking him out in 90 seconds.

FIGHT FIVE

DATE 5 November 1989
VENUE Royal Albert Hall, London
WEIGHT 16 st. 6¾ lb.
OPPONENT Melvin Epps, New York – 13 st. 11¾ lb.
RESULT DQ 2
SUMMARY The outpunched American is disqualified for refusing to obey the referee's orders.

FIGHT SIX

DATE   18 December 1989
VENUE   Kitchener Auditorium, Ontario
WEIGHT   16 st. 4 lb.
OPPONENT   Greg Gorrell, Kansas – 14 st. 2 lb.
RESULT   TKO 5
SUMMARY   Lewis goes to his home town for his first fight in Canada. He floors Gorell in the first 30 seconds, but has to wait until the fifth for the referee to intervene.

FIGHT SEVEN

DATE   31 January 1990
VENUE   York Hall, Bethnal Green
WEIGHT   16 st. 10 lb.
OPPONENT   Noel Quarless, Liverpool – 15 st. 11½ lb.
RESULT   TKO 2
SUMMARY   Lewis opens up with his big punches in round two and floors Quarless twice before the end.

FIGHT EIGHT

DATE   22 March 1990
VENUE   Leisure Centre, Gateshead
WEIGHT   16 st. 9¼ lb.
OPPONENT   Calvin Jones, Ohio – 17 st. 5¼ lb.
RESULT   KO 1
SUMMARY   The American hits the deck twice, the second time for the full count.

FIGHT NINE

DATE 14 April 1990
VENUE Royal Albert Hall, London
WEIGHT 16 st. 9¼ lb.
OPPONENT Mike Simuwelu, Zambia – 16 st. 5 lb.
RESULT KO 1
SUMMARY The Zambian is knocked out inside a minute by a right-hander followed by a left hook in his own corner.

FIGHT TEN

DATE 9 May 1990
VENUE Royal Albert Hall, London
WEIGHT 16 st. 8½ lb.
OPPONENT Jorge Descola, Argentina – 15 st. 13½ lb.
RESULT KO 1
SUMMARY Descola is knocked to the floor inside ten seconds and is finally counted out at the end of the round.

FIGHT ELEVEN

DATE 20 May 1990
VENUE City Hall, Sheffield
WEIGHT 16 st. 6½ lb.
OPPONENT Dan Murphy, Nebraska – 15 st. 0¾ lb.
RESULT TKO 6
SUMMARY Lewis's longest fight yet. Murphy gets on his bike for five rounds until caught by two right-handers in the sixth, when the referee intervenes.

FIGHT TWELVE

DATE   27 June 1990
VENUE   Royal Albert Hall, London
WEIGHT   16 st.
OPPONENT   Ossie Ocasio, Puerto Rico – 16 st. 5 lb.
RESULT   Win on points, eight rounds
SUMMARY   The wily former world cruiserweight champ becomes the first man to take Lewis the distance – teaching him a few tricks as he does so.

FIGHT THIRTEEN

DATE   11 July 1990
VENUE   Superstars Nite Club, Mississauga, Ontario
WEIGHT   16 st. 4 lb.
OPPONENT   Mike Acey, West Virginia – 16 st. 11 lb.
RESULT   KO 2
SUMMARY   The American is floored twice in each round, with the fight ending after 92 seconds of round two.

FIGHT FOURTEEN

DATE   31 October 1990
VENUE   National Sports Centre, Crystal Palace
WEIGHT   16 st. 0½ lb.
OPPONENT   Jean-Maurice Chanet, France – 14 st. 9¾ lb.
RESULT   TKO 6
SUMMARY   Lewis wins his first title – the European belt – by outclassing the ageing champion.

FIGHT FIFTEEN

DATE	6 March 1991
VENUE	Wembley Arena, London
WEIGHT	16 st. 3 lb.
OPPONENT	Gary Mason, London – 16 st. 11 lb.
RESULT	TKO 7
SUMMARY	Lewis's first fight against a world-rated opponent sees him become a double champion. He sends Mason into retirement and picks up the British belt.

FIGHT SIXTEEN

DATE	12 July 1991
VENUE	Caesar's, Tahoe, California
WEIGHT	16 st. 1 lb.
OPPONENT	Mike Weaver, California – 15 st. 5 lb.
RESULT	KO 6
SUMMARY	A muted performance by Lewis until an explosive right-hander delivers the knockout.

FIGHT SEVENTEEN

DATE	30 September 1991
VENUE	Royal Albert Hall, London
WEIGHT	16 st. 7 lb.
OPPONENT	Glenn McCrory, Co. Durham – 15 st. 11 lb.
RESULT	KO 2
SUMMARY	In this defence of his British and European titles, Lewis overpowers the former cruiserweight world champ. McCrory is floored twice and counted out as he tries to rise.

FIGHT EIGHTEEN

DATE 23 November 1991
VENUE Omni Arena, Atlanta, Georgia
WEIGHT 16 st. 6½ lb.
OPPONENT Tyrell Biggs, Philadelphia – 16 st. 7 lb.
RESULT TKO 3
SUMMARY Biggs had beaten Lewis in the 1984 Olympic quarter-finals, but is no match for him here. Lewis ends it in the third, after flooring Biggs three times.

FIGHT NINETEEN

DATE 1 February 1992
VENUE Caesar's Palace, Las Vegas
WEIGHT 16 st. 1 lb.
OPPONENT Levi Billups, California – 16 st. 4 lb.
RESULT Win on points, ten rounds
SUMMARY Lewis goes ten rounds for the first time in his Las Vegas début. Billups is awkward, but Lewis has a clear win: 100–90, 99–91, 98–92.

FIGHT TWENTY

DATE 30 April 1992
VENUE Royal Albert Hall, London
WEIGHT 16 st. 6½ lb.
OPPONENT Derek Williams, London – 16 st. 9 lb.
RESULT TKO 3
SUMMARY A triple-title showdown. Lewis adds Williams's Commonwealth belt to his collection when he floors him with upper-cuts in the third.

FIGHT TWENTY-ONE

DATE   11 August 1992
VENUE   Hurrah's Casino, Atlantic City
WEIGHT   16 st. 9 lb.
OPPONENT   Mike Dixon, Tennessee – 14 st. 11 lb.
RESULT   TKO 4
SUMMARY   Lewis does as he pleases for three rounds before becoming the first man to stop Dixon, in the fourth.

FIGHT TWENTY-TWO

DATE   31 October 1992
VENUE   Earls Court Arena, London
WEIGHT   16 st. 3½ lb.
OPPONENT   Donovan 'Razor' Ruddock, Toronto – 16 st. 7½ lb.
RESULT   KO 2
SUMMARY   Lewis shakes the boxing pundits by destroying the man thought to be the most dangerous active heavyweight in the world. Ruddock is floored at the end of the first and twice in the second. Victory results in the WBC subsequently awarding Lewis its title, stripped from Riddick Bowe when he backs out of an agreement to meet the winner of this fight.

FIGHT TWENTY-THREE

DATE   8 May 1993
VENUE   Thomas and Mack Center, Las Vegas
WEIGHT   15 st. 10 lb.
OPPONENT Tony Tucker, Tyler, Texas – 16 st. 4 lb.
RESULT   Win on points, twelve rounds
SUMMARY   In spite of a damaged right hand, Lewis retains his
          WBC title. He floors Tucker twice on his way to a
          unanimous points win over the man who had lost only
          once (to Mike Tyson) in forty-eight fights.